The Promise of a New Day

About the authors:

Karen Casey is the author of several very popular meditation books, including *A Woman's Spirit, Daily Meditations for Practicing the Course*, and *A Life of My Own. Each Day a New Beginning*, her first book, inspired this one. Although writing is her first love, Karen has also taught elementary school and college and has been a publishing executive. She is married and has a Ph.D. in American studies.

Martha Vanceburg has worked in theater, advertising, public relations, publishing, and academia, but prefers writing. She is married to her best critic and has three children.

The Promise of a New Day

A Book of Daily Meditations

❧

Karen Casey *and* Martha Vanceburg

A HAZELDEN BOOK

HarperSanFrancisco
An Imprint of HarperCollinsPublishers

HarperCollins Web Site: http://www.harpercollins.com

HarperCollins®, 🏭®, and HarperSanFrancisco™ are trademarks of HarperCollins Publishers Inc.

FIRST HarperCollins PAPERBACK EDITION PUBLISHED IN 1984.

FIRST HarperCollins MASS MARKET EDITION PUBLISHED IN 1996.

ISBN 0-06-255268-6

An Earlier Edition of This Book Was Cataloged as Follows:
ISBN 0-86683-502-4 (pbk.)

05 06 ❖ BANTA 10 9 8 7 6 5 4

Introduction

It takes strength to step enthusiastically into each day of our lives. This strength comes more readily on some days than on others, but every day makes demands on us.

Personal experience has taught us that centering ourselves in the face of these demands smooths our passage. To get centered means to sense our place in the grand scheme and to trust the rightness of all experiences that beckon.

It is our hope that these brief daily meditations will help you find your place and thus help you summon the forces to see you through the days ahead. We both follow a Twelve Step program for sane living, and openness is an integral part of this approach. Healing, help, and wisdom may come from anywhere, so we gathered these quotations from men and women of many lands and times, and let them stimulate our own reflections.

Taking responsibility for our own lives, trusting in the rightness of a plan—however we may define the higher power that is its source—and nurturing ourselves to be the best we can; these are the tasks that renew our energies even as we perform them.

The words we have chosen remind us that women and men in every place and time have pondered, struggled, succeeded, and failed in much the same way as we. In every case, they had the drive to begin their journeys anew, day after day. They are like all of us. We are like all of them: journeying forth courageously one day, tentatively the next. The real importance of the journey is simply that we're making it, alone and yet mysteriously together.

—the authors

January

One faces the future with one's past.
—Pearl S. Buck

We are never divorced from our past. We are in company with it forever, and it acquaints us with the present. Our responses today reflect our experiences yesterday. And those roots lie in the past.

Every day is offering us preparation for the future, for the lessons to come, without which we'd not offer our full measure to the design which contains the development of us all.

Our experiences, past and present, are not coincidental. We will be introduced to those experiences that are consistent with our talents and the right lessons designated for the part we are requested to play in life. We can remember that no experiences will attract us that are beyond our capabilities to handle.

All is well. I'm ready for whatever comes today. My yesterdays have prepared me.

*One cannot collect all the beautiful shells on the beach,
one can collect only a few.*
                                        —Anne Morrow Lindbergh

Our lives are a series of selections. We select
projects to do, activities to participate in,
friendships to cultivate. And often we'll have
to forego some of the selections we've made
because time and energy run out. Full commitment, total involvement with singular activities and few friendships, is far better than
partial attention to many. Rapt attention to
the moment and all of whatever it contains
enriches our lives; nothing less than full attention can do so.

   The talents we each have been blessed with
can only be developed if we use them fully to
benefit the lives of others as well as our own.
Thus, when our selections are vast, our attention is sporadic and our talents aren't fully developed. The fullness of our lives individually
and collectively is proportionate to the depth
of the relationships developed between ourselves, our friends, and our activities.

*I can't be everywhere today. Nor can I attend
to the needs of everybody I meet. I will carefully choose where to give my attention and
then offer it totally.*

January 3

. . . goodness cannot adopt the form of blind passions, even in the act of defense and offense, and even when it refuses to tolerate evil. . . .

—Benedetto Croce

Willful blindness can't be good. To shut out any sight from the mind's eye is to exclude part of life. Any action blindly taken is likely to do unintentional harm.

It's not easy, when we're in the grip of any strong feeling, to stop ourselves from acting on blind impulse. It's not easy, but it's wise. Yielding to an impulse, without giving ourselves time to "see" it through clearly, can set us up for guilt or regret.

We needn't know everything in order to act; we merely need to know ourselves. "Blind passion" hides most of ourselves from view. Passion may move us to great selflessness, but never to great clarity, and good actions come from the clear-seeing soul.

I can trust myself to mistrust blind passion, and to wait for clarity before I take action.

Faith is not, contrary to the usual ideas, something that turns out to be right or wrong, like a gambler's bet; it's an act, an intention, a project, something that makes you, in leaping into the future, go so far, far, far ahead that you shoot clean out of time and right into Eternity, which is not the end of time or a whole lot of time or unending time, but timelessness, that old Eternal Now.

—Joanna Russ

Isn't it amazing how some people contrive to live in the present? They seem not to worry about the future; they seem not to regret the past. "Two days I can't do anything about," runs the saying, "yesterday and tomorrow."

We love to fantasize about the past and the future: What if Napoleon had died in infancy? Where would I travel in a time machine? But we get into trouble when we forget that "the past" and "the future" are inventions; the only reality is the present. Yes, past events contribute to our now; yes, the present will help to determine the future. But we can't do anything about them; the past and the future are out of our reach.

It seems, oddly enough, that it's people with a strong faith who are best able to live in the present moment. Enjoyment of the present, care for the quality of life: these are a kind of reverence, a kind of faith in life itself. The present is valuable, this faith tells us: it is all we have.

Let me swim in the present, reverential and unafraid. Let me be sustained by the water of life.

January 5

Nothing on earth consumes a man more completely than the passion of resentment.
— Friedrich Nietzsche

Our obsession with controlling other people, and our failure to succeed with our attempts, are most likely consistent attempts, the fodder for the resentments that we garner. It's human to want to control others, to try to control outcomes to favor us. But the resentment that develops begins controlling us, and this situation leads only to frustration, at times panic, always unhappiness.

If we're feeling resentment toward anyone, or because of any situation, we are not able to recognize the opportunities presenting themselves to us today. And when we don't respond to the invitations for meaningful involvement, our personal growth is jeopardized.

We give our power away when resentment swallows us. Our identity becomes enmeshed with it. Responsible action eludes us. Fortunately, we can take back our power just as soon as we decide to get free of the resentment.

The lesson I must learn is simply that my control is limited to my own behavior, my own attitudes. Today can be my new beginning.

It is not what we see and touch or that which others do for us which makes us happy; it is that which we think and feel and do, first for the other fellow and then for ourselves.
—Helen Keller

Our attention to someone else's needs is spirit-lifting, both for that someone and for ourselves. We need to move our focus away from the self to experience our well-deserved emotional health. The more frequently we honor another person's needs above our own, the greater will be our own strides along the path to health and wholeness.

When we peer beyond ourselves, we remove our attention from whatever our present personal problem is and it dies from neglect. We keep a problem a problem when we indulge it by obsessing over it. Switching our focus offers a perspective that's new, and thus destined to be beneficial.

All around me today are people whose needs are greater than my own. Personal health is enhanced when I forget myself.

January 7

I'm not sorry for anyone's being poor; I'm only sorry when they have no work.

—Helena Morley

Human beings have been described as animals with language, animals with laughter, tool-using animals, animals that play. But we're pre-eminently animals that work. Small children's play is imitation of the work they see adults doing. Fortunate adults put the same energy and devotion into their work as children do into their play.

Work—although we sometimes curse it—is a blessing. Work, the work that is a real expression of the spirit, focuses our energy and allows us to be whole. Maybe our real work isn't our job; maybe we feel whole when we're carpentering or cooking or writing, and we think of these as "hobbies" or "just stuff I do." If we could bring to our jobs the concentration and pride with which we turn a chair leg or roll up sticky buns, we would exalt our working days.

The jobs we do, the work for which we're paid, are deeply important to most of us. When we find work we can love, and do it as well as we're able, we've earned a victory in life.

I will try to be able to say of my work today, "I would do this even if I weren't paid for it."

*All writers are vain, selfish and lazy, and at the very
bottom of their motives there lies a mystery.*
                                    —George Orwell

For the most part, we receive too much information. We're bombarded with print, sound, images. Many of us cultivate a healthy skepticism: we consider the source. What does this person, this agency, this network, this advertiser, or this elected official stand to gain from telling me this information?

But we cannot doubt everything. Humans need to believe in something, even something wildly implausible on the face of it. Thus, cults and causes abound. In this age of widespread corruption and cynicism, faith also is widespread.

Faith is healthy; it is an affirmation of human worth and continuity. Fortunate are those of us who have both strong faith and good judgment. Belief in the essential goodness of our fellows and in the basic rightness of our world can renew our vitality and remind us to treat others with the respect due their humanity. In turn, others will respect our belief in them.

Sometimes, faith is betrayed; sometimes, we stumble. But the delusions or mistakes of others need not sour us; they are part of the mystery.

*I will believe in my own capacity for goodness,
and all will be well.*

January 9

When a man leaves off believing in imaginary property, then only will he make use of his true property.
                                        —Leo Tolstoy

The original meaning of property is "belonging to the self." In this sense, land, houses, money, paintings, jewels, cars, cannot be our *property;* they are all things, and we enjoy using them, but they have nothing to do with our *selves.*

What then is our true property? It's our moral and spiritual qualities; our capacity for love, our commitment to honesty. These are what make a difference in who we are. The difference between a lie and the truth is vastly greater than the difference between a bicycle and a Mercedes. When we appreciate this distinction, we can begin to develop our spiritual selves.

We all know that things can't make us happy; only a loving heart and a clear conscience can do that. Yet often we act as though the piling up of things was important in itself. A little reflection can restore our balance and return our imaginary property to its true place in our lives.

True property is what nothing can take away from me.

*A private railroad car is not an acquired taste. One takes
to it immediately.*

—Eleanor R. Belmont

The hunger for solitude visits each of us at
various points in our development as whole,
healthy human beings. It's in our solitude that
we come to know ourselves, to appreciate the
many nuances that distinguish us from others.
It's in the stillness that we detect our soul's in-
clinations. The privacy of silence offers us the
answers we need. The distractions that stood
in our way no longer fetter us when we've invited solitude to be our guest.

We need time away from others, from the
chaos of our job, families, and society if we
are to find, once again, the clarity we need to
make the best forward movement. We cannot
hear "The Director" call to us when all around
is the clatter of voices and anxiety.

*I will relish the moments of silence today.
They'll reward me with sure guidance and
clarity of thought.*

Children require guidance and sympathy far more than instruction.

        —Anne Sullivan

Children are not just the people under ten. We are all children at heart. And in many of the activities that call us we are as uncertain of the steps to take, as unsure of the course of the outcomes as any ten-year-old. No matter the age, what we all need in the midst of any challenge is soft comfort from a loved one and gently probing questions that serve to guide our choices as we move ahead with the task.

Giving someone explicit directions about how to proceed can deprive them of opportunities for discovery. Stumbling is part of the human experience. Picking ourselves up allows us an additional glance at the landscape on which we tripped. In the second glance comes a new understanding and thus the growth the gift of life has promised us.

I'll comfort another child today and willingly accept the guidance offered by my own mentor.

Freedom means choosing your burden.
                    —Hephzibah Menuhin

Every one of us is haunted by fears of some
measure. That we learn through pain and
grow beyond our fears we can only appreciate
in retrospect. During the moment of painful
confrontation or the spell of overwhelming
anxiety we learn only that we're feeling no joy,
no peace, and probably no security. However,
we must remember that no painful burden,
be it immobilizing anxiety or a relationship
in which we've become victimized, has "happened" to us without acceptance—no matter
how passive. We are free to reject all burdens
and all unhealthy conditions. That we don't
relish our freedom from all pain is a fact of the
human condition.

Looking anew at the struggles that con-
found us and accepting responsibility for them
doesn't lessen them, perhaps, but it does restore our personal power. We are not powerless, worthless individuals at the mercy of our
friends and coworkers. We are in partnership
all the way, and any moment we each have the
power to rewrite the terms of the contract.

*I am free today to be who I want to be. To grow
or not to grow. To feel joy or pain.*

January 13

*Our reality is influenced by our notions about reality,
regardless of the nature of those notions.*
                              —Joseph Chilton Pearce

How we greet today will color the returns
of this day. Further, our expectations will be
manifest, which means we have the personal
power to determine the course our minds and
thus our actions will take. It's both awesome
and thrilling to understand that we are each
responsible for our affairs. Moreover, we will
handle them with ease or experience turmoil
as is our habit.

What we perceive at any moment is equal
to our vision of that moment. If we want more
laughter, greater freedom, further attainments,
they lie within our power—they can't elude us
unless we let them. But first we must define
our direction for movement and then coach
our steps along the way.

*I go where I want to go. I see what I want to
see. Everything can change in a flash of the
mind's eye.*

Perhaps this very instant is your time . . . your own, your peculiar, your promised and presaged moment, out of all moments forever.

—Louise Bogan

"This very instant" is all we have. We make plans for the future, we invoke memories of the past, but really, all we have to deal with and to act in is the moment at hand. We cannot stop its going; we cannot hurry the next moment on its way. Like everyone else in the world, we're partners in the dull, humdrum, dazzling, fabulous, totally unpredictable moment.

And if we have a time that is "our time," it's right now. It has to be, because there isn't any other. Maybe we've had times in the past that were special for us; maybe the future will hold precious moments. But the only time that is truly "our time" is this time, where we are, right now. And what we do with this time is ours to decide.

Each moment is mine, to make as beautiful or as painful as I choose.

*When the most important things in our life happen we
quite often do not know, at the moment, what is going on.*
—C. S. Lewis

Retrospect offers us what no one moment,
in the present, is capable of doing. There is
a pattern to the events of our lives, and even
what appear as the most inconsequential occurrences are contributing their input to the
larger picture that's developing. There is no
question but that every event has meaning.
No experience is without its impact. Time
will reveal the reason for the baffling or troubling situations that have dogged our paths
along the way.

Whenever the road feels rocky or we are
confused, we need to trust. Our lives are not
happenstance. There is a performance being
staged.

How helpful it is to understand that we are
all "players" sharing the same stage. All of us
are needed for some acts, and there will be a
concluding scene making clear the intricacies
of our many earlier scenes. As life progresses,
our understanding grows. Our finales are assuredly appropriate to our life plan.

*Today's happenings will have their impact.
Sometime—in some way. All moments, all
events are part of my sacred pathway.*

We are partakers of a common nature, and the same causes that contribute to the benefit of one contribute to the benefit of another.

—William Godwin

Ecology, the study of how all life fits together, has an emotional dimension. We all know people who are emotional polluters. Bullies, gossips, or self-pitiers spread a noxious influence; no one wants to be around them.

Often they're gifted people, and sometimes they're in positions of power over others. It's difficult to keep our own clarity among the belching smokestacks of an emotional polluter. But our ecology—our interconnectedness—means that, potentially, we influence them as much as they influence us. If we can stay out of their poison, refuse to play, we can help to clean up the atmosphere.

Our ordinary notions of politeness often lead us to encourage emotional polluters. We may not see that our tacit acceptance and co-operation harms both us and them. Let us use our faith in our common nature to behave cleanly; we will thereby help others to clean up their acts.

I'll try not to confuse politeness with pollution.

If we seek to be loved—if we expect to be loved—this cannot be accomplished; we will be dependent and grasping, not genuinely loving.

—M. Scott Peck, M.D.

We receive love when we give love, with no strings attached. Bargaining for love is sure to disappoint us. It's human nature, when bargaining for anything, to hope to pay only half of what something is worth. Expressing this attitude in our relationships guarantees that we'll be shortchanged.

No one of us is free from the need for love. And most of us search for reassurances of that love from the significant people in our lives. However, the search will be unending until we come to love ourselves. Love of self is assured when we understand our worth, our actual necessity in the larger picture of the events that touch us all.

When we realize our value and see that life's mysteries have reasons, we'll no longer doubt ourselves and we'll be free to love and understand another's value too. We need never grasp for love when we sense the real meaning of the lives that surround us.

I will love someone fully today and I'll understand their meaning in my life.

The true wonder of the world is available everywhere, in the minutest parts of our bodies, in the vast expanses of the cosmos, and in the interconnectedness of these and all things.

—Michael Stark

Let's take a moment and look around ourselves. All that we see has its connection to us and to all other parts of this vast universe, and there is a universal rhythm with whose beat all life is in tune.

Our existence, all existence, is to be marvelled at. How perfect is the rosebud, the baby's toenails, the dog's sense of direction. We are not alive by accident. The beat of our hearts is necessary to the continued beat of the Universe. The whole is maintained by the combination of all the parts.

Life is sacred, all life. Friends and enemies are sacred. Lovers, children, parents are sacred. When we've come to understand this fact, understand it to the depths of our being, we'll know love; we'll know ourselves. Most of all we'll feel the peace that accompanies faith in the vastness and the rightness of the Universe and all it contains.

Everything as far as my eyes can see and heart can feel is contributing a part to my personal existence today.

Imagine that we conjure up a world that is safe for mothers and daughters.

—Louise Bernikow

The question of violence and danger in society occupies a lot of time, breath, and printer's ink. The possibilities of peace and safety take up very little. It is common for us to think of containing violence by greater violence: the violence of weapons, of prisons, of riot squads. And yet the teachers whose wisdom we prize above all others tell us that one cannot answer force with force; that only peace and detachment can meet violence and draw out its poisons.

No sane person wants war. Yet we are so locked into violent patterns of thinking that many of us believe we should prepare for it. How would we go about preparing for peace? What are the first steps we could take? What is peace, anyhow? We seem to know very little about it.

A world that is safe for mothers and daughters would be safe for fathers and sons as well. Let us search our hearts to discover what we know of peace, and let us talk to one another, work together to realize our knowledge.

I shall not study violence anymore; instead, I shall discover as much as I can about peace and safety—for in my life, peace begins with me.

It is not fair to ask of others what you are not willing to do yourself.

—Eleanor Roosevelt

Equality is a state of mind. When we value our own self-worth, we are comfortable with the achievements and the well-being of our friends and associates. The symptoms of a punctured ego occur when we criticize others and make demands we don't want to fulfill ourselves.

Most of us experience wavering self-confidence on occasion. It may haunt us when a big task faces us. Or it may visit us when we least expect it. It's a facet of the human condition to sometimes lack self-assurance. At times we need to remember that life is purposeful, and the events involving us are by design.

Almost daily we'll face situations we fear are more than we can handle, and we'll hope to pass the task off to another. It's well for us to remember that we're never given a task for which we're not prepared. Nor should we pass on to others those activities we need to experience personally if our growth is to be complete.

I must do my own growing today. If I ask others to do what I should do, I'll not fulfill my part of life's bargain.

Let me listen to me and not to them.
—Gertrude Stein

Our ears would fill with advice, if we listened to it: advertisers, evangelists, publishers, educators, all clamoring to market their products, try to get us to conform to their notions of what we should be.

One of the dangers of a democratic society is confusing the individual and the mass—using statistical data to define persons instead of trends. "Trendiness" is a way of avoiding individuality. To choose for ourselves means taking responsibility for our choices, saying, "I do this because I want to."

Each of us has an interior voice that knows what we want. We know—even if the knowledge sometimes causes us pain—that we're unique individuals, with goals, programs, and behaviors distinct from others'. Acknowledgment and enjoyment of our full humanity means owning our differences—listening to our own voices.

I am the expert on my own life. Today and every day let me be wise enough to consult myself.

All our resolves and decisions are made in a mood or frame of mind which is certain to change.
—Marcel Proust

When we are alert in the here and now we are constant collectors of new information. Consciously and subconsciously we sift through it and file it away—not to be forgotten, however. Our opinions, our attitudes, and our responses to life are influenced and expanded by those moments in which we absorbed new information, moments that in turn enhance our credibility as flexible, thoughtful decision-makers.

It is much easier to keep our minds closed and our attitudes and behavior rigid. Venturing into uncharted territories need never be risked. Each day becomes predictable and dull—in time, not really worth living.

Life's joys lie in adventure. We're promised adventure every moment of the day if we open our eyes to it. The currents that flow from the activities around us are charged with reasons for reformulated plans, new opinions, advanced enlightenment. That we're fully contributing members of the universe is evidenced in our flexibility when called for by changing situations.

I can change my mind today with pride, if new information calls for it.

January 23

No person could save another.
—Joyce Carol Oates

We encounter the experiences we need in our lives. It's sometimes hard to believe that when we're grappling with disappointment, anger, or loss. Yet everything that comes our way is material for our growth.

Many of us entertain a fantasy that some person can complete us. We don't believe that we're complete in ourselves. Only when we do will we become able to share in a life-enhancing partnership with another person. Only when we love ourselves can we love others realistically, instead of seeing them as fantasy figures, projections of our own desire.

No one can hurt us emotionally unless we allow the hurt. We're full partners in everything that we do, and taking responsibility for our actions and our desires is our first step toward being fully lovable.

The only one who can save me is me.

He has the right to criticize who has the heart to help.
—Abraham Lincoln

Our negative judgments of others very frequently inform us of our own shortcomings. In other words, what we dislike in others are often those things we hate about ourselves. Much better than criticizing another's abhorrent behavior is a decision to look inwardly at our own collection of traits and attitudes. Our desire to criticize, to pass judgment, offers an excellent mirror of who we truly are. And the image we see reflected can guide our movements toward becoming healthier, happy individuals.

We can feel a bit of gladness for what our negative reactions are able to teach us—but we must be willing to learn from them. How exciting to contemplate that every hateful moment actually is offering us a positive opportunity for change.

It's human to find fault, and we shouldn't be overcome with shame. However, we hinder our own personal growth every time we quickly criticize another rather than rejoicing that we've been given an additional opportunity to move closer to the person we're being called to become.

Today I'll look beyond others' faults and recognize my own.

January 25

Is there any stab as deep as wondering where and how much you failed those you loved?
— Florida Scott Maxwell

Treating our loved ones as we hope to be treated is our assurance against failing them. And if we listen to our inner voice, we'll never falter in our actions toward others. There is always a right behavior, a thoughtful response, a respectful posture.

Let us be mindful that we're sharing our experiences with others who need the talents we have to offer. It's not by coincidence but by design that we're given opportunities to treat those close at hand in some manner. We'd do well to let the choice be loving.

How we treat another invites like treatment. Actions from our heart will soften our own struggles. Also, spiteful, critical treatment of others will hamper our steps. We teach others how to treat us by our gestures and words.

The inner voice can be heard if I choose to listen. It will never guide me wrongly.

I came into this world, not chiefly to make this a good place to live in, but to live in it, be it good or bad.
—Henry David Thoreau

To live is to open ourselves to possibility, to rule out nothing. There is no way we can spare ourselves, or those we love, the pains of living, because they are inseparable from the joys. How grandiose we are when we think we can save the world.

All we can do—and it's quite a lot—is to live the best way we can, achieving a balance amid the forces that pull on us: pleasure, responsibility, power, love. If we can live so that we respond to all of them, rule out none of them and yet enslave ourselves to none, we will have the best the world can give.

One quality all great people seem to share is humor—the capacity to see our struggles and triumphs with detachment. Not that our life is unimportant, but that it's only a part of the huge web of life on this planet.

If we can keep our lives in balance, we won't get puffed up by any little triumph, or squashed by a defeat. We'll keep on with our lives, confident that we're doing our best.

Let me not forget—my chief business in life is living.

January 27

I feel we have picked each other from the crowd as fellow travelers, for neither of us is to the other's personality the end-all and the be-all.

—Joanna Field

It's not mere chance that we gravitate toward those who become our friends. Nor is it only happenstance that we are piqued by others. We are, in fact, on a journey and have much to learn. From our friends and even more so from those not so friendly, we are destined to learn what our souls yearn for. The journey is the process of enlightenment for which we all have gathered. From one another we are receiving that which we're ready to learn. All of us students. Each of us a teacher.

How comforting to know that the pain of a particular experience, or the confusion over a set of circumstances, will become understandable with the passage of time. All experience plays its part. All of our acquaintances share destinies overlapping our own. There is security in knowing that our journeys are necessary and right for us.

I'll not discount the value of any person or any experience that circumstances offer today.

A truth that's told with bad intent
Beats all the lies you can invent.

—William Blake

The quality of our relationships with others depends heavily on our motives. If we're trying to change our friends, to correct their behavior or to improve their lives, we'll ensure a poor quality of friendship.

The only life we have power over is our own. Trying to fix other people isn't only futile, it's disrespectful. Chronic "fixers" are likely to attract people who seem to cry out for their services. Over time, the situation usually proves to be a set-up for frustration and anger.

Self-respect begins inside ourselves. Real consideration for others demands that we treat them with the same respect we'd like to receive.

There is no such thing as my telling someone something "for their own good."

January 29

I come from nothing, but from where come the undying thoughts I bear?

—Alice Meynell

Nothing is new under the sun, except each day as it dawns. The thoughts that visit our brains have all been thought before; the freshest, brightest, best ideas and inventions all have their roots in ancient visions of human possibility.

Yet this day is new because it is our January 29. The elements that make it up may be immortal. They have not ever come together in just this way before. We feel at home in the timelessness of our spirits and the sense of the unique possibilities of today. We will be given many chances, today, to be the person we want to be.

We have no power over the events of today, except our power over our own behavior. If we act from our knowledge of what is right for us, all will be well.

I am unique, and I have inherited the rich medium of thought.

Maturity is the capacity to withstand ego-destroying experiences, and not lose one's perspective in the ego-building experiences.

—Robert K. Greenleaf

Our emotional health is proportionate to our willingness to take personal responsibility for thoughtful responses to the myriad circumstances in our lives. We are not powerless over our attitudes or over behaviors, even though we are generally powerless over the events themselves. The most troubling of times need not diminish us, unless we let them.

Likewise, the flavor of the most pleasurable situation retains its long life in proportion to our willingness to assimilate the experience gradually, letting it enrich us but not overwhelm us. Overreaction to any event casts a spell over us, inhibiting our ability to perceive accurately the moments, hours, perhaps even days of experiences that follow.

Finding the balance between overly emotional reactions to people and circumstances and disinterested passivity takes effort and a commitment to emotional health. And that balance is the real key to experiencing a life that's joyful.

No event need throw me today. And yet, every situation offers me a chance to practice healthy living.

It seems to me that in the long run it is impossible to maintain a democratic society unless you can spread the benefits and burdens of being an American citizen reasonably evenly.
—Felix Rohatyn

In our relationships, in our work and play, do we assume an equal share of the burdens, and do we get a reasonable amount of benefits in exchange?

There's no way to calculate the burdens and benefits of living. But our own inner awareness is a pretty accurate measure: if you feel ripped off and resentful, then something's wrong; if you feel guilty, as though you were getting away with murder, something's wrong.

Often we're reluctant to track down the source of our guilt or our resentment; we're afraid that what we find may force us to change the way we live and work, and change is painful.

Letting go of a source of pain can be as difficult as losing a source of pleasure.

I am the only one who knows just what is going on in my life, and all such choices are mine.

February

February 1

You are a child of the universe no less than the trees and the stars; you have a right to be here. And whether or not it is clear to you, no doubt the universe is unfolding as it should.
                                                    —Max Ehrmann

There is a patterned sequence to the events surrounding us, attracting our attention, inviting our personal involvement. We must accept this as a given, and then attune ourselves to the rhythm of the ordered flow. This will augment our personal growth and facilitate our contributions, which are both needed by other players in this sequence of events.

We need not understand the full picture of the pattern we're each woven into. We need only trust that it's a design which will comfort us—if not today, then tomorrow.

I can go forth today—sure that events will move me in the right direction even though I can't see what's around the corner. There will be no unplanned event in the big picture.

. . . we ourselves are only fragments of existence, and our lived life does not fill the whole of our capacity to feel and to conceive.

—Paul Valéry

Our feelings are bigger than we are. The love, sorrow, fear, or rage that any one of us feels at any moment is just a thin slice of a great stream of feeling that runs through all of humanity. To experience strong emotions in a crowd, for instance, takes us out of ourselves.

Mob anger can be viciously destructive. Mob joy can be transcendent. The difference between one individual and the mob is that each of us can choose, every moment, what we will do with our emotions. We can feel rage and choose to express it without harm. We can feel sorrow and survive it. We can choose to dwell with feelings that console and enhance our spirits, and we can choose to let go of those that diminish us.

With feelings, as with everything else, the law of life is change. We shall not always feel as we feel now. If we accept our feelings as they come, and try to feel them fully as we're able, we shall become more unified with our fellow human creatures, and with all existence.

Pressure builds up behind a dam. I will let my feelings flow.

February 3

. . . fear makes strangers of people who should be friends.
                            —Shirley MacLaine

Life is sterile and stifled when we close ourselves off from the smiles or swift glances of
others. The opportunities we have for personal contacts are not mere chance. We draw
to ourselves experiences and thus acquaintances which will lend meaning to our lives.

Our fear of others is generally tied to our
sense of personal inadequacy. How frequent
are our suspicions that others are smarter,
more capable, destined for greater success.
However, we fail to gain the growth promised
by another's presence in our lives when we
give in to the fears that haunt us all at times.
Those strangers in our lives are not without
purpose. Their growth, as well as our own, is
dependent on the removal of the barriers separating us.

*A stranger lingering in my life is not here by
chance. I will gain from opening myself.*

No one can make you feel inferior without your consent.
— Eleanor Roosevelt

Self-talk is powerful. It will develop a healthy ego. Likewise, it can trigger ego deterioration. Our strength in times of trouble can be doubled or eroded depending on the commitment we've made to positive self-worth.

A secure self-image and unwavering self-confidence are characteristics we all long for. They need not elude us; they are our birthright. However, most of us fail to understand we need only to claim them to own them. Instead, we doubt our abilities, question our self-worth, and discover that our strength and our potential are exactly what we think they are.

Belief in ourselves precedes achievement. Our successes are always within our power if we understand our responsibility for them. We are self-talking every moment; the words we use are our personal choice.

I'll be conscious today of my self-talk. My experiences will directly reflect my thoughts.

February 5

It's important to know that words don't move mountains. Work, exacting work moves mountains.
—Danilo Dolci

Exercising our spiritual muscles for the arduous and exacting work of faith is a new thing for many of us. Our culture doesn't seem to put the same value on spiritual power as it does on muscles or intellect. Yet a strong and agile spirit, the kind that can do the work that moves mountains, is possible for us all.

Like the muscles of our arms and legs, the spirit swells and grows with use. Small acts of faith will show us the way. As we grow increasingly secure, we are capable of greater and greater leaps of faith. Real prayer, real meditation, means touching and using that inner core of faith, and the more we do it, the stronger it grows.

The fullest life is possible for those whose powers are the best developed. If we choose to move mountains, we must be prepared to work. Even achieving freedom of choice in our lives means developing our spirits.

My spiritual power matches the task at hand. As I become stronger, I can accomplish greater things.

In this world everything changes except good deeds and bad deeds; these follow you as the shadows follow the body.
                                        —Ruth Benedict

Our identity, our being at any moment, is a composite of all we have been in the past. Some of our actions have made us wiser. Others haunt us because we didn't put forth our best effort. All of our deeds contributed in some measure to our growth, however, and they can guide our choice to behave honorably today.

Acceptance of who we are, our total self, is necessary for our emotional maturity. Shame for past actions will keep us stuck. Our restitution for the past is best made by responsible behavior today. How fortunate that each waking moment offers us opportunities to become our better selves.

Today, just like every day, I'll make choices to behave in ways that will fill me with pride or shame. I pray for thoughtfulness today.

February 7

With history piling up so fast, almost every day is the anniversary of something awful.

—Joe Brainard

"History" is mostly a record of awful events—war, famine, conspiracy, oppression, betrayal. But surely, every day is equally the anniversary of something wonderful. It's all in how you look at it.

Perhaps a calendar of wonderful anniversaries would be an antidote to depression: this is the day I first heard tender words from someone dear; this is the day I stopped smoking; ten years ago on this day I committed myself to a program of positive living and spiritual growth.

Keeping such a calendar, even for a short time, gives us a record of spiritual progress. Even to be able to say, "How different I am from what I was five years ago" can be a truly cheering thing. Why let the tyranny of history depress our spirits? Let's make our own.

I will treasure the private record; the public one will keep track of disasters.

He who angers you, conquers you!
—Elizabeth Kenny

It's by choice that we let others control our emotions. When we make that choice we have abdicated our personal responsibility for growth. Deciding to feel how we truly want to feel rather than giving someone else control is freeing, exhilarating, and nourishing.

When we let someone anger us, we have decided to make them the object of our attention, and any intention to do what needs to be done is gone. Anger consumes us. With it we become preoccupied and the growth and contributions we were created for come to a standstill. Our personal power to think creatively and to take action are lost when we choose anger instead. For this way, the object of our anger decides who we are.

Today I'll be in charge of my growth if I choose to determine my own emotions.

Imagine there's no country. It isn't hard to do. Nothing to kill or die for. And no religion, too.
                                                            —John Lennon

If we let go of all conventions of life as we know it—the laws, religions, customs, and other institutions—we could train our imagination to build new ones, perhaps based on different values of work and wealth and play.

What is our image of an ideal society? Perhaps it is one in which there is no money. Or one where all work is done by computers and people are free to play. Perhaps our model is military or tribal.

How would we define crime or punishment in our Utopia? What would be the criteria for success and failure? Would we redefine the family as we know it? How would we reward our heroes? Whatever our ideal society is, it's likely to express our most deeply held values.

To find out what I hold most precious, I will try to imagine giving it up.

Limited expectations yield only limited results.
— Susan Laurson Willig

Our thoughts determine our actions, and when our thoughts are negative, our successes are few. What we hold in our mind is certain to be reflected in the day's activities. And we are capable of fueling our thoughts positively, if we choose to.

Positive self-assessment and uplifting pep talks can become habitual if our desire to live up to our potential is great enough. The expectations we privately harbor, be they small or far-reaching, will set the pace for the progress we make today, and every day.

We can greet a challenge with eager anticipation when we've grown accustomed to believing in our capability for success. First, we must expect to handle, with poise, whatever confronts us.

No one but me determines my course today.
My success begins in my mind.

SERVICE. A beautiful word fallen upon bad days.
                              —Claude McKay

Silver service; military service; tennis service; evening service. The word has so many different connotations that we lose the thread that connects them; something done *for another*. Whether it's our profession or our gift, service is our offering of skill or care to a fellow being.

We now have the term self-service, which mostly connotes convenience in shopping. Do we ever truly serve ourselves, in the sense of offering our best to our own benefit? A high quality of self-service is an important part of self-esteem. By taking time for ourselves, treating ourselves gently, we demonstrate our belief that we deserve love.

Quality self-service doesn't only mean caring for our bodies, although that's important. It also means forgiving ourselves, letting mistakes remain in the past, and nourishing our spirits with good thoughts, good words, good deeds. If we're to earn tranquility and joy in life, surely we can learn to serve ourselves with kindness.

Today will abound with opportunities to serve myself and others. I'll be open to them.

For have you not perceived that imitations, whether of bodily gestures, tones of voice, or modes of thought, if they be persevered in from an early age, are apt to grow into habits and a second nature?

—Plato

What does it mean to act "as if"? When we feel angry and unforgiving, it means we act *as if* we forgave someone who stepped on our toes, or took our parking place, or ruined our paintbrush; when we feel cold and self-pitying, it means to act *as if* we were warmly interested in the child or friend or spouse who has something to tell us. It can be a wonderful exercise. If we really give ourselves to the performance, we can act *as if*, and the mood we imitate becomes real.

Oscars will never be given for acting *as if*, but the rewards are far more useful. Acting *as if* can salvage a bad day; it can repair or prevent a quarrel. Act as if we didn't have a headache, and often the headache disappears. Act as if we weren't in a hurry and often we will have time for everything.

When we were small, adults said to us, "Don't make a face or you'll freeze that way." Now that we're grown, we can learn how to imitate, flexibly, what we want. Instead of freezing into negative postures, we reach for agreeable ones—and so often "*as if*" becomes "*as is.*"

Today I shall practice acting as if I were serene; perhaps it will grow into a habit.

February 13

Every truth we see is one to give to the world, not to keep to ourselves alone.
—Elizabeth Cady Stanton

Sometimes we feel that we are the guardians of a fragile, threatened civilization: if it weren't for us, all would be lost. Such feelings are a signal that we need to check out our reality, to test our perceptions of the world against those of someone we trust. We are seldom in sole possession of the truth!

But shared commitment to truth is powerful; it enhances our spirits. Most of us feel a need to express this commitment, whether by sharing worship or simply talking with friends. Often the truth is a process, a relationship between ourselves and others, and sharing it gives it roundness and luster.

I need courage to face the truth; and the truth will strengthen me.

It is not the things we accomplish that are important, it is the very act of living that is truly important.
—Dr. Bill Jackson

We've been invited to participate in this life, to be present, one to another, and that's all that's expected of us. Our successes may bring us personal joy, but our value as persons lies only in our being.

But living fully is more than just making an appearance, here—today. It's celebrating our oneness—our ties to one another—our need for one another's presence to complete our own. And we can be a celebrant only when we're involved and fully focused on the experience. We capture life's gifts, its riches, when we are intent on the moment's fullness. We miss what we most need when our hearts and minds are distracted.

All that's asked of me is rapt attention here, now, to others. And I'll find the good life.

I had often occasion to notice the use that was made of fragments and small opportunities in Cranford. . . . Things that many would despise, and actions which it seemed scarcely worthwhile to perform, were all attended to. . . .
—Elizabeth Gaskell

Our lives are full of "fragments and small opportunities." Bouquets of wild grasses, shells and pebbles from the shore, a half-hour visit to a convalescent home, small acts of kindness, found poems—anything that enriches the moment, for ourselves or for another, is worth performing.

And it's the busiest people who seem to have time for these fragments, time to smell the flowers. It's often a shock to realize that doing something nice for ourselves might involve a small deliberate kindness to another. But the more we are good to ourselves in this way, the richer our lives become.

The moment is mine to cherish and to share. When I share a kindness, I double it.

You can't cross a chasm in two steps.

—Rashi Fein

When a small child hides her eyes, she means, "You can't see me." We sophisticated grown-ups sometimes have trouble getting rid of magic thinking. We tear petals from daisies, one by one; we tell ourselves that anything we eat standing up has no calories. We know one must leap across a chasm, but still we think, "If only I could change feet in the middle!"

The important thing is getting to the other side—tackling the problem on its own terms. Playing magic games is one way to stay stuck. There's nothing romantic or admirable about futile efforts; they're an admission that we don't want to succeed.

Every problem teaches us how to resolve it. If we can't see the solution, then we're not ready for it, and instead of sputtering vainly we should set that question aside and address ourselves to our appropriate tasks.

I will remember that wishing almost never makes it so. Wishing and working almost always do.

. . . concern should drive us into action and not into depression.

> —Karen Horney

If a situation in our lives causes concern, be it mild disgruntlement or serious frustration, we should understand that our concern indicates that we need to act, responsibly. Events that attract our attention need our action.

Our actions can take many forms. Occasionally we will be called upon to take charge of a situation. More often, offering emotional support to another is all that's needed. Perhaps most frequently, our prayers are enough.

There is always a proper response to any circumstance that causes us concern. If we choose no response, our inaction will only heighten our concern. And preoccupation will hinder the day's activities.

My actions today should reflect my concerns and be appropriate to the need.

If the only tool you have is a hammer, you tend to see every problem as a nail.

—Abraham Maslow

When we can take a long view of our problems, we can sometimes see that we're using inappropriate tools to try to solve them. What's necessary for us to do is to move away, to detach. That may show us a whole new context into which our problem fits—and in which it may not even be a problem.

Detachment is hard to achieve when we're deeply hooked into a situation. When we send ourselves drastic messages like "now or never!" we're pressing our noses right up against the problem—a position in which it's difficult to maintain a balanced view. To stop and say, "If not now, then perhaps some other time," unhooks us and lets us remember that life is richer and more varied than we thought when we were hooked.

Crisis thinking can be like a hammer—it flattens everything. This can be our way of trying to control the outcome of our individual struggle. But when we remember that we make up only small parts of one grand and beautiful design, we can surrender our problems to it.

To be a competent worker, I will seek out the tools that are best suited to my task.

February 19

Eyes, what are they? Colored glass,
Where reflections come and pass.
Open windows—by them sit
Beauty, Learning, Love, and Wit.
                              —Mary Elizabeth Coleridge

How we appear in others' eyes can become an obsession. Do they see me as I see myself? Or do they see the Real Me—and is that worse, or better? Are the eyes of others mirrors, in which I'll find my own reflection? Or are they windows, through which I can touch the spirits of those I love?

We can never know the real lives of others, but we can trust that they are not so different from our own. The experiences we share are more powerful than those in which we differ; others struggle with the same temptations and surrender to the same destiny as we do.

If we esteem ourselves, we won't worry about others' opinions. Of course we want to be respected, loved by those we love, accepted as a fellow traveler on life's journey. But our main concern is our own spiritual growth— and it will be the key to how we are perceived.

Today, I'll look within and seek to please myself.

Do not dream of influencing other people. . . . Think of things in themselves.

—Virginia Woolf

One sort of plan is doomed to almost certain failure: the plan we have for someone else. An experienced breeder can predict a pedigreed puppy's future with reasonable accuracy, but a human child is quite a different matter. Any relationship that is built on our expectations for another turns into a bitter struggle, a disappointment, or both.

There is one person, and only one, on whose life we can have a strong, positive influence, and that is each one of us. What's more, we deserve our own support. We'll richly repay our efforts in our own behalf. Anything we can do for ourselves will stay with us; the more we learn, the wiser we'll become.

"Things in themselves" are the actual things in our lives, now: our work, our play, our relationships, our spiritual growth. These things deserve our best efforts. As we become more and more the persons we want to be, we will discover the spheres we are meant to inhabit, and learn to welcome those who share them with us.

My efforts in my own behalf are never wasted.

Although the act of nurturing another's spiritual growth has the effect of nurturing one's own, a major characteristic of genuine love is that the distinction between oneself and the other is always maintained and preserved.
                                        —M. Scott Peck, M.D.

Those we love must be free to love us in return, or leave us. The honest evidence of our love is our commitment to encouraging another's full development. We are interdependent personalities who need one another's presence in order to fulfill our destiny. And yet, we are also separate individuals. We must come to terms with our struggles alone.

One gift of life available to each of us is security, the sense that accompanies the recognition of our spiritual center. Helping someone else discover their spiritual gifts strengthens our own. Nothing is too difficult when we act in unison as separate entities, relying on the spiritual core that strengthens us to meet any situation.

My own spiritual center will be strengthened if I help someone else develop theirs.

Happiness is the meaning and the purpose of life, the whole aim and end of human existence.

—Aristotle

We find happiness with our friends, if we expect it there. The workplace guarantees it, too, if we go in search of it. Happiness visits us in our solitude and in our myriad involvements. Wherever we are, so is happiness, unless we've chosen to keep it out. Our attitudes are powerful, and will prevail in all matters, with all people.

Happiness is contagious. It spreads quickly when shared freely. When it catches up with us, the cares of the day are immediately lightened. We have lessons to learn in this life, and we have essential contributions to make, contributions that will ease another's burdens, foster happiness in another's heart. Likewise, someone else's lessons may well encourage our own happiness.

Every struggle is eased by laughter. I am never left to struggle alone, unless by choice. Today will be joyful and eventful if I live in the laughter.

February 23

When we think of cruelty, we must try to remember the stupidity, the envy, the frustration from which it has arisen.

—Edith Sitwell

Our outer behavior matches our inner state of mind and emotional well-being. Our expectations of others are consistent with our personal expectations. When we feel less than adequate because of our imperfections, we treat others like failures, too. How someone treats us today indicates how that person feels about herself or himself.

Self-love is lacking wherever people criticize others destructively, and self-love is necessary before we can offer love to any of the people in our lives. Developing self-love requires discipline. Our existence verifies our value as human beings. Understanding that our lives do have purpose contributes to our ability to love ourselves.

Today is day one for me to develop my loving behavior.

If you shut your door to all errors, truth will be shut out.
                              —Rabindranath Tagore

Since so much of the world remains mysterious, how can we rule out new possibilities? It's very human to want to cling to the little bits of truth we're sure of; but we mustn't use those bits of knowledge to keep us from the possibility of further discoveries.

True wisdom includes the humility to acknowledge what we don't know. The careful scientist and the experienced physician are humble before the immensity of what they don't know.

New experiences, new relations and connections can reveal more and more, if we are open to them. Once we decide we know something—and close our minds to the possibility that we don't—we're keeping ourselves willfully ignorant. Filtering out life's richness robs us of our birthright—experience. Nothing is true that can't stand to be tested against life's flow.

Even welcome visitors can only enter through a door I've opened.

February 25

Relationships are only as alive as the people engaging in them.
                                    —Donald B. Ardell

We receive from every experience in proportion to what we give. In other words, the richness of our lives is necessarily dependent on the depth of our commitment. Reserved involvement guarantees only limited rewards, while wholehearted efforts promise full-scale returns. In all aspects of our lives, we'll find this to be true.

Our relationships gift us justly. These experiences with others are woven together, and their beauty is equal to the beauty we bring to one another's company. However, if we bring only criticism and bleak hopelessness to a relationship, we'll find despair rather than joy. Every relationship is the sum and substance of the partners involved. No relationship is more fruitful than the efforts of those doing the pruning.

How much do I give to the relationships I deem meaningful? They bless me in just proportion to what I give. Today gives me a chance to make a greater contribution.

Self-determination does not mean exercising intellectual mastery at all times over bodily, earthly processes, though the capacity for that mastery expands our human possibilities.

—Linda Gordon

Growth means learning the limits of our will. What appears to be mastery—flying in an airplane, for example—is merely cooperation with natural forces. Human intellect does not *master* natural processes; we tap into them, learn them, bring our own aims into harmony with them.

The world is not a jungle, to be hacked, cleared, or bulldozed. Human beings are learning not to clear jungles that way either. The world is us extended over the globe. We can spend our whole lives discovering the wonderful oneness of creation.

The awareness of this unity expands our human possibility, for each case is an example of our growing harmony with nature.

I will pray for harmonious resolution of my human possibilities with the great forces of nature.

February 27

God creates. People rearrange.
                                    —Joseph Casey

Being alive is our invitation to act in fresh, inventive ways. All it takes is concentrating on our inner vision in combination with external reality. The components for accomplishing any task are at our fingertips, awaiting discovery.

Our burdens are lightened when we understand that all situations are resolvable—no mystery need leave us in the dark for long. Just as surely as we each exist, so exists every element we need to solve any problem or chart any new course. Our purpose in life is to select those elements that will satisfy the need. We each have been blessed with this capability for proper selection.

The day promises challenge and many choices. I can successfully handle all possibilities.

I want somehow to tell the story of how the dispossessed become possessed of their own history without losing sight, without forgetting the meaning or the nature of their journey.

—Sherley Anne Williams

To use the past without being controlled by it—that is our responsibility to history. Because the past is irrecoverably vanished, it's sometimes tempting to forget it or to falsify it. But being true to ourselves means being true to our history.

Past cruelties can remain powerful in our lives—yet to take possession of our history means to free ourselves of bondage to past events. Nothing can ever change them. If we are to make the future good, we'll learn what the past can teach us. But our freedom requires us to make choices based on the needs of the present, not the past.

I can act at every moment in such a way as to honor the past and enhance the future.

February 29

Patience is a particular requirement. Without it you can destroy in an hour what it might take you weeks to repair.
—Charlie W. Shedd

Enjoying the moment, in its fullest, makes possible a peaceful and patient pace. Progress is guaranteed if our minds are centered, in the present, on the only event deserving of our attention. We can be certain that error and frustration will haunt us if our attentions are divided.

Patience will see us through a troubled time, but how much easier it is to savor patience when it's accompanied by faith. We can know and fully trust that all is well—that our lives are on course—that individual experiences are exactly what we need at this moment. However, faith makes the knowing easier and the softness of the patient heart eases us through the times of challenge and uncertainty.

Patience slows me down long enough to notice another, and to be grateful for the gifts of the moment. Patience promises me the power to move forward with purpose. Today's fruits will be in proportion to my patience.

March

March 1

It is time to show the strength of water and flow away. . . .
To stand is to be crushed, but to flow out is to gather new
strength.

—Marge Piercy

Water is one of the strongest elements on earth: it can't be broken; it can assume many shapes; it joins easily with itself. When it reaches a certain mass, moving water presents an irresistible force.

We might do well to learn to acquire the strength of water temporarily; to be able to lose ourselves for a time, in concert with others, and then to reclaim our identities. We needn't fear their loss. We are unique personalities, and our selfhood is intact.

How successful I would be if I could use the
strength of water when I need it; the purity
of air, the solidity of earth, and the appetite
of fire.

One's mind may be given readily and it may be given with zest. Not all control is oppression. Sometimes it is release.
—Gilbert Ryle

Our most dangerous delusion is that we can control others. The hard-won truth is that we can control only ourselves—and it may take us a lifetime to learn this. Self-control means release, however; release from the bondage of uncontrolled and thoughtless behavior. When we recognize that our only legitimate power is over ourselves, we become free to grow spiritually and to increase that power.

Lack of control is not freedom; it is chaos. Conflicting impulses squander energies instead of controlling them and directing them toward growth. We can't subdue our unruly selves by fighting them: accept them, love them as part of our human imperfection, our superb and jagged individuality.

As we come to recognize the benefits of self-control, we'll choose it more and more often. We'll become more fully in control of our lives, better able to direct our energies and do what we want to do.

Only by choosing self-control will I achieve freedom.

March 3

Love is mutually feeding each other, not one living on another like a ghoul.

—Bessie Head

Real love is compromise. It's sharing and taking turns. It's putting someone else's best interests first. Love wears many expressions and is demonstrated by many gestures. Offering love to someone, when the offer is genuine, benefits the giver as much as the receiver. Our calloused souls are softened by the gentle nature of our love. No one of us develops mentally and emotionally to our full stature if we cultivate isolation rather than intimacy.

We learn who we are through our involvement with others. We come to terms with our defects and have opportunities to enhance our assets while experiencing the strengths and shortcomings of others. What time and patience teach is that love is generally slow to develop but will result when there is a mutual decision to live and grow in one another's company. Each person we genuinely love makes our own survival easier.

My love is best expressed when I help someone else live life more comfortably.

The art of pleasing consists in being pleased.
                                    —William Hazlitt

Others' pleasure in our company becomes our pleasure. If we can set aside our self-conscious anxieties and simply enjoy being with others, they will enjoy us. As lovers know, there is no aphrodisiac like a loved one's desire.

When we give one another our full attention, we enhance one another's humanity. Much of life consists of routine transactions, in which people hardly recognize each other as human. Even intimate relationships can come to suffer if we withhold ourselves.

When we discover pleasure in each other's company, we kindle a spark of joy that illuminates far more than the moment.

Today I will decide to be fully human in all my encounters.

March 5

. . . you don't get to choose how you're going to die, or when. You can only decide how you're going to live. Now.
                                        —Joan Baez

The responsibility we each are charged with for our individual development is awesome, particularly when we look ahead to our whole life stretching before us. It's not uncommon to be immobilized with the fear of making a wrong decision, heading down a dead-end path. It's with great relief that we realize that the tomorrows will take care of themselves if today is well lived.

Lives well lived, a hope that's cherished by us all, are not beyond our simple grasp. Attention to the demands of the moment only, coupled with the decision to behave in ways that will fill us with pride, will ensure that our experiences are generally smooth. The attitude we carry into any situation will influence the outcome, our growth, but most of all the quality of our whole lives.

I need to concern myself with today, only. And live it well.

"Freedom ain't nothing but knowing how to say what's up in your head."

—Ralph Ellison

The freedom to speak our minds is a precious gift. Throughout the world, throughout history, it has been and is a rare privilege. The privilege should oblige us in return to broaden and strengthen our minds, so that what we speak is worthy of free people.

The obligation is not to be perfect; the search for truth proceeds by trial and error. It is to be generous, forgiving, and honest. A moment's thought before we speak might save us and those around us many petty words.

We can't choose our feelings. From time to time we'll be swept by feelings that we wouldn't choose. But we can choose our actions. We can always choose to speak or not. Often it's wiser not to speak out of negative feelings. If we remind ourselves that free speech was a hard-won right, we may have more respect for the way we enjoy it.

A moment's reflection may keep me from abusing my rights—or others'.

March 7

Nothing happens to any man that he is not formed by nature to bear.

—Marcus Aurelius Antoninus

Reflecting on the past reveals that indeed we do find the strength and the ability to cope with whatever experiences ripple our calm. Moreover, we have come to accept that the tides of turmoil wash in new awareness, heightened perceptions, measurable calm.

Tragedies are guaranteed to trigger first pain, then perceptible growth, and finally, tranquility. Over and over again we pass through these stages that are designed to nurture our fuller development as healthy human beings. Over and over we see that the tough times teach us what we're ready to learn.

We can look to the day ahead fully expecting to be strengthened enough to handle whatever we've been readied to experience. Nothing will present itself that can't be coped with.

Today I can be certain of growing. I will meet the challenges in unison with my inner strength.

*". . . you never get over bein' a child long's you have
a mother to go to."*

—Sarah Orne Jewett

For most of us, our mothers were the first
love, and the quality of our relationships
throughout life is influenced by that earliest
one. A mark of real maturity is the ability to
see our mothers simply as human beings—
lovable, fallible, interesting, and imperfect,
just like ourselves.

Some or us have suffered a mother's early
death; some of us cope bravely with her long
illness. Few of us have a simple, easy relationship with our mothers. Too much is at stake.
The infant who needs its mother's arms lives
on within us all.

Few of us have such a continuous bond with
our mothers, but we're fortunate if we can have
an adult relationship that includes the love and
nurturing we crave, because we never get past
the need for it. The most successful intimacy
seems to be based on reciprocal nurturing, for
we need to give as well as to receive.

*The child I was lives within me, and so does the
mothering caretaker I first loved.*

All great reforms require one to dare a lot to win a little.
　　　　　　　　　—William L. O'Neill

Unfortunately, life does not come with a money-back guarantee. Going after what we want, especially if we're up against established interests, is likely to demand the commitment of our best energies—with no certainty of getting it.

Oddly enough, some of the happiest people we are ever likely to meet are those who devote their lives to seemingly hopeless causes. For such people, daring a lot can mean staking their lives on a belief. The outcomes are bound to be small in proportion: failure, perhaps. At best, limited achievement.

But none of this seems to matter. In fact, a happy person with a cause seems to have totally let go of the outcome. The joy is in the struggle, in the process. They learn so much; and by living for something outside themselves, their own small problems miraculously fall into line.

Today I'll keep in mind that achievement is risky, but dedication wonderfully liberating.

One cannot have wisdom without living life.
—Dorothy McCall

Understanding circumstances, other people, even ourselves comes with the passage of time and our willingness to be open to all the lessons contained within a moment. We must be willing to participate fully in the events that have requested our attendance. Then we can discover the longed-for clarity about life and our role in it. Immersion in the moment accompanied by reflective quiet times promises a perspective that offers us wisdom.

We all long for happiness, an easier life, and wisdom. We learn so slowly that both happiness and the easier life are generally matters of attitude. Therein lies our sought-after wisdom. How much simpler it makes living through even our most feared experiences when we have acquired the wisdom to know that the mind we carry into the moment, any moment, will be reflected in the outcome.

It takes patience and willingness to live fully enough to reap the benefits that accompany wisdom.

Today I'll practice patience.

What most of us want is to be heard, to communicate.
—Dory Previn

The need to know that we count in the lives of others, that our presence has not gone unnoticed, is universal. Few of us are blessed from birth with full knowledge of our connectedness to all life. Instead, we falter and fumble our way through our experiences, uncertain of our worth and meaning. Acceptance by others is our want. Unconditional love is our due.

Since we all share this same need to be acknowledged, it's best we each offer acknowledgement to those sharing our experiences today. They aren't unlike us; their needs and insecurities match our own. We'd all survive the harsh bumps of life with so much greater ease if we felt the comfort of others. In the company of others nothing is too much for any one of us to handle.

Today I'll remember that others need my comfort and willingness to listen just as much as I need theirs.

There are two tragedies in life. One is not to get your heart's desire. The other is to get it.
—George Bernard Shaw

Desire is strong; we all feel it. Desire can impel us toward positive, life-enhancing experiences, or it can fasten on vain and unproductive ends. Material things will never satisfy desire; only a serene spirit and a detachment from outcomes will enable us to live peaceably beside the torrent that is our desire.

In itself, desire is neither good nor bad. How we direct our desire, and whether we join it to our love or to our anger, determines the effect it will have in our lives.

If our desire is continually unfulfilled, perhaps we should examine, deeply and honestly, the direction we've allowed it to take. If achieving our desire leaves us feeling hollow, we should do the same. Desire can nourish us if we understand it as a continuous process, a part of our spiritual growth.

Let me be sure that what I desire is worthy of my best self.

The best thing for you, my children, is to serve God from your heart, without falsehood or shame, not giving out to people that you are one thing while, God forbid, in your heart you are another.

—Glückel of Hameln

We pray for wholeness of the spirit: to be able to live cleanly, with no shame, and to meet every aspect of life with the same serene face. It isn't easy for most of us. We fuss. We trip ourselves up. We may find ourselves telling lies, creating emotional turmoil to escape what we see as even greater turmoil.

The first step toward wholeness is for us to admit that we are human. No, not perfect; yes, about as flawed as everybody else. Once the knowledge is part of us that we're part of suffering, seeking humanity, a lot of falsehood and turmoil shears away.

There isn't any big secret to protect; there's just you, just me. However different we may appear, we're more than kin. And we can keep each other honest. The habit of honesty, once formed, is harder to break than the habit of lying.

I shall resolve to show the same face everywhere, and I'll become serene.

*My children weary me. I can only see them as defective
adults . . .*

— Evelyn Waugh

If we expect children to behave as adults, of
course we will find them tiresome. If we expect water to be milk, we will be continually
disappointed. But—since we can control and
direct our expectations—why should we set
ourselves up for such inevitable annoyances?

But we do. We are constantly expecting
things unreasonably, and then being disappointed, shocked, heartbroken, and betrayed.
It would be so much more rational simply to
take things as they come, without expectations.

But that would involve a degree of detachment that most of us would find impossible—
even repulsive. It would mean unhooking our
feelings from other people's behavior. "But I
care about her," we say. "Of course I want her
to . . ." It doesn't much matter what we want
her to do; get married, get divorced, brush her
teeth at night, or come in before midnight.

What matters is our involvement, our expectations. We can care about her and still not
feel hurt by her actions that may not be what
we want. Hurtful actions are another matter;
but she has a right to be who she is, just as we
all do.

My expectations today will be only for myself.

Gold, for the instant, lost its luster in his eyes, for there were countless treasures of the heart which it could never purchase.

—Charles Dickens

The mysterious thing about "treasures of the heart" is that they are "countless"—boundless, self-renewing, inexhaustible. When we love and are loved, trust and are trusted, this reciprocal relationship gives us and those who love and trust us a literally endless wealth.

Only when the relationship is one-sided do we feel drained by our commitments. Love that is based on mutual understanding and respect will never drain us of our resources; our fund of love is replenished even as it flows out of us, as though the act of loving generates more love.

Fear can impede this miraculous process. In general, we have to know ourselves pretty well and be quite secure in our own skins before we can make to someone else the glad and unconditional gift of ourselves. Love entails risk—the risk of being completely open, and completely self-forgetful. But all success involves risk; and in this case the rewards are the greatest possible.

I will not let fear keep me from the treasures of the heart.

Within our dreams and aspirations we find our opportunities.

—Sue Atchley Ebaugh

Our dreams invite us to broaden our horizons to reach beyond our present goals. They are much more than whims. They are probably calling us to those opportunities for which our talents have been readied. Most of us need this encouragement to attempt new ventures.

We've each been invited to this present moment by design. Our lives are joined like the tiles of a mosaic; none of us contributes the whole of the picture but each of us is necessary for its completion. More importantly, the depth, the richness of the picture in its entirety, is enhanced by our fulfilled dreams.

With joy and excitement we can anticipate our frequent aspirations, recognizing them as the guideposts offering directions for our daily travels.

Today I will welcome my dreams. They indicate tomorrow's successful ventures.

Every outlook, desirable or undesirable, remains possible for anyone, no matter what his present outlook is.
—Dr. George Weinberg

The attitude with which we greet the day, approach a situation, or respond to a friend or co-worker is fully within our control. We exercise absolute control over little in our lives, but our attitudes represent personal choice each moment.

Recognizing the power inherent in personal choice is exhilarating. It means we are free from domination by others, if such is our choice. Freedom to act, to think, to dream our own dreams is ours when we exercise it.

I celebrate my power today. I am free to choose my every response to each encounter. Hallelujah!

Life is curious when it is reduced to its essentials.
—Jean Rhys

Life is always reduced to its essentials. We're frail creatures: without water and shelter, we can't survive. We may not think of our lives in these minimalist terms, but accidents of many kinds can disrupt our fragile web of protection.

It makes sense, then, to assure ourselves of the best quality of life while we have it. This does not mean luxury or plenty; a high quality of life accompanies a high standard of behavior and relationships.

Clarity and honesty in our dealings with others will assure the quality of our lives. Simplicity is more satisfying than complexity. The less we get in our own way, the more clearly we can see these elegant essentials of life—elegant in that they are never extraneous. Life is indeed curious in the way it engages our full attention.

Like a curious child, life presents me with the most interesting questions. I'll be patient, and the answers will come.

We are apt to call barbarous whatever departs widely from our own taste and apprehension. But soon [we] find the epithet of reproach retorted on us.

—David Hume

Judging others is a hazardous game that's likely to backfire. Labeling others is a form of judgment. It's a way of sticking people into pigeonholes and saving ourselves the effort of thought. Do we really want to be thoughtlessly tossed by others into some category not of our choosing?

The world's rich texture holds much that each of us will love, and much to which we'll be indifferent. How much more pleasant it is to look for—and to find—what we like, than to sneer at and judge what we don't. A need to judge others is a sign that we lack confidence in our own taste—an indication of shaky self-esteem.

Our personal growth asks us to look positively at life. We want to find occasions for rejoicing, not disapproving. The thoughtless and intolerant teach others that they themselves are not worthy of respect.

I will set aside my judgment of others and concentrate instead on freeing myself.

. . . you must remember that an arbitrary power is like most other things which are very hard, very liable to be broken.

—Abigail Adams

Sway is built into tall buildings so they won't break. Rigid structures are never as strong as flexible ones. The strongest minds are also the most nimble, the most ready to change and to include new information.

We only see one little slice of reality. How can we know what's right for others? Our spirits will be strong to the extent that we can keep them flexible, ready to incorporate new energies and to make fresh associations.

To be flexible doesn't mean to be wishy-washy or indecisive; often people who refuse to grow will say they want to "remain flexible." But one can be flexible and still have strong direction, generosity, and broad tolerance for others' growth. What cannot bend may break.

I'll respect the truth of your living, growing spirit. Your reality can be your gift to me.

March 21

If our species does destroy itself, it will be a death in the cradle—a case of infant mortality.
                                            —Jonathan Schell

Compared to rocks or to termites or ginkgo trees, our whole species is a very recent passenger on this Spaceship Earth. We've had a busy time of it, for the few thousand years that there have been enough of us to make a difference. But in time as geologists measure it we have barely entered the history of the planet.

If we eradicated ourselves with the lethal means at our disposal, we wouldn't be the first species to disappear. But wouldn't it be a shame? We humans have the capacity for transcendence as well as destruction. Surely we're adaptable enough to guide our own development away from our current preoccupation with deadly toys.

Written history gives us just a tiny glimpse of life on earth. Let's live so as to guarantee that human existence lasts out its full chapter.

I am one of the earth's children. I will treat my parent with respect.

It is good to have an end to journey towards; but it is the journey that matters, in the end.
                                  —Ursula K. LeGuin

Our goals lend direction to our lives. Without them we flounder, often uncertain of who we are. They provide substance for our self-definition and they motivate us, at times even deeply exhilarate us. Nevertheless, it's the many steps, the myriad activities, the unexpected barriers along the daily journey that give real meaning to our lives. We are so much more than our completed achievements, and the process is what develops the person within.

It's far too easy for most of us to miss the moment and its richness because our sights are on a particular journey's end. How often do we fail to appreciate the many occasions for feeling satisfaction over a task well done? We seldom grasp the full joy of living because our sights are glued to the future.

It is a hard but easily forgotten lesson that a goal completed is always followed by a letdown. The joy resides in the process.

Can I stay with the moment and the activity before me, just for today?

When I trust and respect myself enough to be myself honestly, others respond with trust and respect.
—John Stevens

We can greet all situations today with ease if we have committed ourselves to lives of integrity. Having made the decision to be fully honest at all times eliminates our uncertainty in responding to others, and thus we don't cloud issues and confuse our contemporaries with inconsistencies.

Without fail we recognize others' integrity as ours is recognized. It goes without saying that each of us is more at ease with those we trust.

Honesty invites honesty. Self-respect encourages respectful behavior toward others, and like a boomerang, it returns to the initiator. We teach others how to treat us. With every action we take, every word we speak, we are informing others of our personhood.

I will set the tone for my day by my behavior toward self and others. Over this I am all-powerful.

*Being human is itself difficult, and therefore all kinds
of settlements (except dream cities) have problems.*
—Jane Jacobs

A sure cure for rage at the minor irritations of
daily life is to sit back from the traffic jam, the
broken appointment, the lost vital information, and say, "Being human is itself difficult."
It may not cure our frustrations for long, but
it's worth practicing.

Many of our troubles stem from forgetting
just how difficult it is. We often have impossibly high standards for behavior, especially our
own. We are complicated, marvelous creatures
who have many skills, but we thwart our own
capacity for enjoyment by expecting that we
will be perfect.

Being human is difficult; we perform it im-
perfectly. And when we combine our effort
with others'—building a building, performing
a play—we multiply our imperfections as well
as our skills. Yet we need each other.

If we can detach ourselves from anger and
disappointment and reflect on how wonderful
it is that we can do anything at all, we may remember to love ourselves and others for our
human complexity and simplicity.

*Nobody's perfect; such is the nature of my
humanity.*

March 25

. . . we will be victorious if we have not forgotten how to learn.

— Rosa Luxemburg

There is no goal beyond our grasp, no achievement beyond our attainment if we reduce our natural barriers against new information and new perspectives. Our victories accompany perseverance, fearless learning, openness to the unfamiliar.

Each of us is experiencing a particular period with a select group of people, by design, not by chance. Myriad situations call us, and messages secure our attention because they contribute to our potential for victory. What's asked of us is rapt attention to the moment, intense openness to its richness, and a willingness to be edified or humored or perhaps simply nurtured. We will gain from every moment's offering whatever we need for our continued growth and ultimate victory.

Learning is forever in my control. The decision is personal and perhaps must be made each day, anew. The choice is mine.

When you have become willing to hide nothing, you will not only be willing to enter into communion but will also understand peace and joy.

—Anonymous

Keeping secrets is synonymous with keeping stuck. Our human potential is stifled by our stuffed feelings, attitudes, ideas. Conversely, the more we allow others to really know us, the greater will be our opportunities for growth and happiness. Our secrets burden us.

The choice to shield our inner selves from others is ours to make. Risking vulnerability takes strength, and a great deal of courage. We can never be certain that our audience won't betray us. However, we can be certain that words and thoughts hidden will haunt us.

The gift of total honesty and openness is profound intimacy. It's this gift that makes possible a level of friendship that dispels self-doubts, that gives rise to a euphoria that turns all situations into opportunities for greater happiness.

I may be tempted to keep some secrets today. I will remember that sharing them will relieve me of a burden that weighs me down.

. . . we do not always like what is good for us in this world.
—Eleanor Roosevelt

Today will call each of us to make our particular contributions to the moment. There is no guarantee that we will enjoy every experience, but we can be certain each one of them will teach us something we're ready to learn because "when the student is ready, the teacher appears."

Little reflection is necessary for us to realize that our most troubling times have generally been responsible for our greatest growth. Our achievements are always accompanied by periods of frustration, occasional loss of direction, even momentary despair because the actual results miss the mark of our hopes. However, the passage of time makes clear that these actual results benefit us far more than those we'd hoped for.

Our personal vision is narrow and limiting. We can't really imagine what's in store for us. The most we can do is trust that our experiences have our best interests in tow.

I'll remember: Today I'm a student and my experiences are my teachers.

The person who fears to try is thus enslaved.
—Leonard E. Read

Immobilization is fear's result. In its grip we fail to move forward. We fail to think new thoughts, live new experiences, chance new personalities. All that life is prepared to offer us goes ungreeted.

Let us remember, we have been given the gift of life and we are obliged to test our wings and spring forth, displaying the message that's within. Even when fear crouches close at our heels, we can elude its grasp if we remember this message that eternally accompanies us: "All is well."

Life is a series of opportunities for emotional, spiritual, and intellectual growth. No opportunity for action is beyond our capabilities.

I will look to this day only. I will be invited to participate in those experiences designed for my particular development. All is well.

March 29

A house is no home unless it contains food and fire for the mind as well as for the body.
—Margaret Fuller

No matter how full our social and professional lives are, we all need a base, a place where we are at home. Whether it's a studio apartment furnished from secondhand stores and garage sales or a luxurious country retreat, one of our basic human urges is the need to make a home. And our spiritual fulfillment asks that our home nourish us.

Look around: in our choices for our home we reveal what nourishes and inspires us. Perhaps we opt for the comfortable and well-used: old books, chairs that speak more to the back and bottom than to the eye. Perhaps we are restless and change the way our homes look frequently. We all use our homes to express our desires.

Are we neglecting "food and fire for the mind"? Sometimes we misinterpret inertia as comfort. Are we giving our minds a wholesome environment?

Fuel for my spirit is never wholly consumed. Today, I will look to my supply.

If you can imagine it, you can achieve it.
If you can dream it, you can become it.
—William Arthur Ward

Our dreams and our aspirations are our invitations to set new goals, attempt new tasks, dare to travel uncharted courses. We each have gifts to offer our fellow-travelers, but most frequently need encouragement to recognize our own strengths and talents.

Seldom do we rise in the morning fully eager to join in the opportunities that await us. More likely we have to prepare our minds, center our emotional selves, nurture the inner person who may fear the experiences the day promises.

It's normal—completely human—to be conscious of our incompetencies while lacking awareness of our abilities. To them we give scant attention, generally blocking out the praise they elicit. To our failings, however small, we compulsively devote our attentive minds. We forget that today's abilities were last year's incompetencies.

Achievements today will be many, and they are indications of past dreams. My hopes today guide me toward future achievements. My failings are few and help to keep me on track.

March 31

Freedom is like taking a bath—you have to keep doing it every day!

—Flo Kennedy

Nothing stands still. Change is the law of life. We may sometimes feel that our personal gains have to be won over and over again. But looked at from another perspective, that's not so: our solid personal gains are the ones that no one and nothing can take away from us.

They are tools for continued growth. Jobs, lovers, houses may change, but serenity and freedom of spirit are within our power to achieve—to maintain—or to give away.

Freedom means choice; our choice of what we do with our bodies, our money, our lives. If we decline to choose, the choice will be made for us. If we don't use or claim our freedom, we are giving it away. Our lives need our active, creative participation every moment.

Like bathing, I must daily exercise my freedom. No one can do it for me.

April

April 1

In the transformation and growth of all things, every bud and feature has its proper form.

—Fritjof Capra

Our lives are a series of unfoldings. Our struggle to be perfect at every stage of life is a common element of the human condition. What comes with age and wisdom is acceptance of our imperfections. We see that we develop at every stage of life.

We can rejoice that we're unfolding according to the needs of our existence. Each day is ushering in new growth, subtle changes. Our transformation is lifelong and according to specifications known to the inner self—our connection to Universal Wisdom.

The changes we'll experience today are compatible with the new growth we adapted to yesterday. And likewise, what will come next week, next year will have been prepared for by the tiny transformations accumulated on this road to maturity. We are developing exactly as we need to each step of the way. And our fit, yours and mine, one with another, is perfect at every moment.

I am changing, growing, maturing at every moment—according to plan.

We must assist natural processes that serve the function of reunification.

—Joseph G. Hancock

Some families in mild climates have begun to experiment with unified living: recycling wastes, growing food, and using only renewable sources like the sun and the wind for power. Seen from the twelfth floor of an apartment building, in sub-zero weather, this is a radical gesture. Yet it's a conservative way of living, asking for little, spoiling nothing, and putting back into the earth everything that's taken out.

We can all put back what we take out, but are we as careful of our emotional and spiritual processes? Or do we sometimes block them or try to erase them or hoard them up? The universe is one sphere. Energy flows through it, through polar bears and bacteria and Republicans and cranberries. Surrendering to the flow is our only way of achieving personal reunification.

I can assist natural processes by giving my assent, freely choosing unity.

April 3

Time is a dressmaker specializing in alterations.
                                            —Faith Baldwin

We are learning as we go, and the experiences shed light on our own plans for proceeding. The steps we are taking, in unison as well as on separate but parallel paths, enhance the particular movements of us all.

We often expect perfection from ourselves, forgetting that we're all beginners in life. The best we can do is willingly acknowledge our errors, grateful that we can always begin again on any task—grateful that we have the experiences of others to help guide us.

Life is process. We learn, we grow, share burdens, reformulate ideas, and restructure our values. Every change we make alters the steps we take, altering in turn someone else's movements, too.

Today I'll discover a change I need to make, one that will reach further than my own task.

He was the victim of his own rage. . . .
　　　　　　　　　　　　　—Paule Marshall

Our negative behavior always turns on us. So
does our positive behavior. Obviously, it's better to have joy and peace rebound on us than
violence. Then why don't we consistently act
peaceful and joyous?

It probably takes an idiot or a saint to be
consistently positive in this world of cynicism,
cruelty, and corruption. However we may
strive to free ourselves of preoccupation with
things beyond our control, we all find ourselves reacting to certain events with rage,
envy, fear, or other painful, destructive emotions. But knowing we have a choice can free
us from bondage to this pain.

We can choose to respond ragefully or envi-
ously—or we can choose to feel the feeling
and then to let it go, so that the negative feeling doesn't control our behavior. Successful
living involves learning to control how we behave; if we hide or deny our feelings, they're
with us forever. It's only by letting them go
that we can be truly free. And it's only by experiencing them that we can let them go.

*I can only spread joy if I stop being a victim
of my own despair.*

April 5

If you would be loved, love and be lovable.
—Benjamin Franklin

We all desire to be loved. Our common human characteristic is our need to count in someone else's life. At least one other person needs us, we tell ourselves, when we feel least able to accept life's demands. How alike we all are. The paradox is that our own need for love is lessened when we bestow it on others. Give it away and it returns. A promise, one we can trust.

The reality about love and its path from sender to receiver and back again is often distant from our minds. More often we stew and become obsessed with the lack of love's evidence in our lives. Why isn't he smiling? Why didn't she care? Has someone more interesting taken our place? Choosing to offer love, rather than to look for it, will influence every experience we have. Life will feel gentler, and the rewards will be many and far-reaching.

Loving others promises me the love I desire. But I can't expect it if I don't give it first.

. . . [I]t was not so much that they drifted, as that in the presence of a boat the world drifted, forgot. The dreamed-about changed places with the dreamer.
—Eudora Welty

Dreams can be so potent and mysterious that many of us, at one time or another, have felt that they put us in touch with some other level of reality. Sometimes we wonder if we're dreaming our waking lives, too. Some of us have had the fantasy that we're characters in someone else's dream, or in some great world-dream.

Sometimes our dreams show us what we want; or what we fear. Dreams are like messages sent from one part of us to another: scrambled messages in which the people, places, and happenings from many epochs of our lives come together.

Sometimes we may dream a great happiness, or a wonderful solution to a problem. Such dreams cast a rosy glow over our whole day; as a nightmare can make us feel uneasy for a long time. Such dreams may be messages about feelings we're not feeling. The dreamed-about—fear or joy—does seem to change places with the dreamers, who have shut the feeling out of their waking lives.

Owning our dreams, cherishing them, is part of fully accepting ourselves. However silly, scary, sexy, or confusing a dream may be, it is our dream, we made it.

I don't need to crack the code to get the message.

April 7

Speak kindly today; when tomorrow comes you will be in practice.

—Anonymous

Behavior is habitual: we thoughtlessly brush our teeth, set our alarm clock, start our car, or dress in order. We create rituals in our lives, and they free us from thousands of small decisions, leaving our minds less cluttered for the more important choices. However, every action we choose sets into motion a behavior that may become habit. We should be wary of habits that harm ourselves or others.

We have the personal power, with every decision, to choose to act in ways that promote well-being—our own and others. For instance, a tense situation might be better served by a smile and a deep breath than by a harsh response. Knowledge of our freedom to choose such a response exhilarates us. We should be mindful that every response that is frequently made is approaching habit, and our habits determine the ease with which we greet and adapt to the conditions life offers.

I am a creature of habit. The power is mine to create positive habits. I will make careful choices today.

I refuse to pronounce the names of possession and non-possession.

—Monique Wittig

New relationships require new names. If we want to stop behaving in a customary way— as an adversary, as a victim, as a bully, as a martyr—then we need new words to describe our new behavior.

Perhaps we glimpse the possibility of a new relationship to power—that one might use power, yet not subjugate others. Perhaps we glimpse the possibility of sharing, of lateral extensions rather than hierarchies.

It's clear that if we are to change the world, we must begin by changing our relations with others. Perhaps we don't want such a grand project as changing the world, but we might want to change old ways of using our skills. Let us be fearless and trust in the knowledge of our hearts.

The only way I can discover the consequences of change is to change.

April 9

Make yourself necessary to someone.
> —Ralph Waldo Emerson

We are each positioned, not by chance but by design, within the context of home, job, friends, and acquaintances. Our involvement with life around us, the myriad experiences that confront us, guides our growth. The gift of life obligates us to contribute our best efforts, our talents to the situations involving us. From them we'll gain exactly those lessons we are ready to handle.

Creation is interdependent. Every element, every human, every organism is necessary to the completion of the whole. How comforting to know that our existence is not mere chance. The space we take here, now, is advancing the development of all aspects of life. We never need to doubt our value, our importance to others. Being alive is the ultimate proof that each of us is necessary to the many persons in our lives. Gratitude for them, and for us, will strengthen our understanding.

I will look upon my many human contacts today with real understanding. I am here by design.

If an idea, I reasoned, were really a valuable one, there must be some way of realizing it.
—Elizabeth Blackwell

These words were written by the first woman who earned a medical degree. They're useful to anyone who fears that their most precious dreams are doomed to failure.

If our dreams are valuable ideas, they will be useful goals. If they're childish fantasies, they won't, although those can be fun. It's important to distinguish the ones we can achieve from the ones we can't. The first kind will nourish us, like bread; the others, like candy, won't.

We have a responsibility to those nourishing dreams, because they come from what's best in us. Our responsibility is to live so that the dream might be realized. When dreams become goals, they have a way of calling us forth. Goals organize our lives, so that we may reach them.

Reaching my goal is never as important as the progress I make toward it.

Happiness is not a matter of events; it depends upon the tides of the mind.

—Alice Meynell

It's all too easy to blame a friend, spouse, or co-worker for the uneven quality of our lives. If only others would behave according to our plans and dictates, then all would go well, we think. What seldom is remembered or even understood is that each of us has an individual perspective on any single event—our own. We need to stretch our minds and hearts to understand an experience from another's point of view. However, we need never fully understand how another perceives life. We need only to accept that another's perspective is legitimate.

Our happiness is not dependent on the perceptions or the actions of someone else. Nor is it dependent on attention, or lack of it, from a loved one. Our occupation may be challenging and fulfilling; however, the joy we get from it depends on the attitude we carry to the job. In every way, whether in the company of others or by ourselves, we make our own happiness.

My opportunity for happiness is guaranteed if I opt for it today.

We must be true inside, true to ourselves, before we can know a truth that is outside us.
—Thomas Merton

Integrity is not a given in everyone's life. It is the result of self-discipline, inner trust, and a decision to be relentlessly honest in our response to all situations in our lives. We are quick to recognize this quality in others, and hope to acquire it ourselves. However, we must cultivate risk-taking and cast off fears of rejection and derision if we're to discover the serenity a fully integral life offers.

Recognition of truth in others, realization of the appropriateness of decisions or the aptness of choices is made easier when we're certain of the truth of our own lives. The inner turmoil dissipates and we are quiet within when we choose to live lives full of truth. And in the quiet we discern all truths. How much softer the edges of experience when we're guided by truth. How much easier every decision, every choice, when we've committed ourselves to a course of total honesty.

My level of peace is my responsibility. I will find just as much as I need.

April 13

You can have your cake and eat it. But my God, it will go rotten inside you.

—D. H. Lawrence

When we try to hang on to another person or to any part of life, we impede the natural flow. To be in harmony, we must let go. "You must lose your life in order to find it." Real strength, real self-respect, is achieved only by setting the hungry self aside.

It's human to want to hold on to what's precious. But life's real treasure is found in achieving the rhythm of ebb and flow. Joy can't be a constant state. Glory is part of a cycle that includes defeat.

Accepting imperfection, accepting change, is part of accepting our humanity. We obey the same cyclic laws that govern the universe. Success in living depends on accepting that one day we'll eat cake and the next we won't. Fear tempts us to hoard the crumbs of our success, but wisdom lets us brush them away.

I will remember that joys recur just as sorrows do.

We must build human relevance into the paradigms of science itself.
—Steven Rose and Hilary Rose

Science itself is not to be feared. We fear what science is capable of—just as we fear what human beings are capable of, when they act on their violent feelings, without control or choice. Science is a powerful tool of the human mind, when it's used with respect and tenderness for the unity of life.

It isn't human relevance we need so much as relevance to this seamless unity. As our capacity for knowledge grows, we glimpse more clearly how interrelated all human efforts are with the great rhythmic processes of the planet. The paradigms of science are the models it makes of the world. When scientists make a model that ignores relevance, they risk using their knowledge stupidly, or harmfully.

We need to recognize that science is part of our human endeavor—not more nor less than art or agriculture or raising children, but part of all of them (as they're all part of science). We must remember how broad a definition of human relevance we need, when we contemplate the unbroken beauty of the world.

There is a choice in all activity; so I will prepare to choose well.

April 15

*Promises that you make to yourself are often like the
Japanese plum tree—they bear no fruit.*
> —Frances Marion

Promises are merely empty words if they aren't
backed up by action. And action is generally
preceded first by deliberate resolve, then ver-
balized commitment (often to someone besides ourselves), and finally, a carefully laid out
plan of steps to be taken. Promises that are
made, but not kept, quickly hamper any progress we dream of making. They hang like
weights on our shoulders, reminding us of our
weak resolve.

Only actions can fulfill our promises. Perhaps we'd do well to make a promise, any
promise, only for a day. We can always renew
it tomorrow.

The additional and unexpected gift is that
a promise kept, no matter its magnitude, enhances our self-image. And since we can only
live one day at a time, no promise need be
made for longer. All of us can manage to fulfill
one promise, for one day, if we believe in it
and in ourselves.

*Today offers me the opportunity I need to feel
better about myself.*

I am ashamed of these tears. And yet
At the extreme of my misfortune
I am ashamed not to shed them.

—Euripides

Shame is a little whip we always carry with us.
We can shame ourselves easily; the little whip
stings. We often use it to punish our feelings,
because they evoke the helpless children we
were. So we learn to suppress our feelings of
fear, or rage, or desire. We would rather not
feel at all than feel the sting of shame.

Why should we punish our feelings? Everyone feels much the same things. Why should
our humanity shame us? Perhaps somewhere
we acquired the notion that it's wrong to be
human; that an inhuman perfection is the only
proper public image.

Love can heal the pain of shame. Self-love
and self-acceptance can make us strong enough
to discard the little whip. We're much more
lovable when we acknowledge our humanity
and let go of our shame. We're also better able
to love others. Shame shuts us up; love opens
us to joy.

I'm grateful for my feelings; they're close to my
capacity for love.

April 17

Noble deeds and hot baths are the best cures for depression.
—Dodie Smith

Preoccupation with ourselves exaggerates whatever condition presently haunts us. The temptation to dwell on our pain is so great, it takes strength and a serious commitment to emotional health to move our focus to another's needs. We are slow to learn that our own pain is soothed each time we offer comfort to another in pain.

Periods of depression will foster compassionate thoughtfulness, if we're willing to take advantage of the natural inertia that accompanies the blues. Our moments of stillness give us time to take note of another's condition. And it's through consideration for another that our wounds are cleansed and healed.

Rarely do we offer rapt attention and sincere concern to the troubled individuals in our lives. And yet, each one traveling our same or parallel pathway needs the attention that only we can give. Our own spirit is nourished every time we offer love to someone else.

Well-being, my own and someone else's, will be fostered by my actions today.

. . . Fatherly and motherly hearts often beat warm and wise in the breasts of bachelor uncles and maiden aunts; and it is my private opinion that these worthy creatures are a beautiful provision of nature for the cherishing of other people's children.

—Louisa Mae Alcott

Nature has beautifully provided that all humans can love all other humans. We don't have to be related by blood, nationality, or even language. Unlike the great apes, we have no unbreakable patterns of rivalry and aggression; we're free to choose love as our means of relating to the world.

Many people choose a sort of great-ape behavior, instead of enjoying the miraculous freedom of their power to cherish others. The choice of mistrust, rivalry, and aggression sometimes threatens to imprison us all in a zoo, surrounded by fences and patrolled by guards.

The choice is ours: can we leave the apes behind? Human love looks risky, from a cage. Let's dare to be human today.

I can choose to bestow the gift of my love.

April 19

The edge of the world does not look far away,
To that I am on my way running.
> —Papago Indian song for a young girl

All things seem possible to us when we're young. The world's problems look solvable; our optimism and our immense youthful energy combine to make us hopeful and impatient. Why didn't anyone see it before? It's all so simple: if people would just love each other . . .

As we grow older, we learn more about the complicated system the world is. We learn that everything is interrelated, and that none of our simple youthful solutions even addressed the problems. In fact, we learn that they aren't problems, they're how the present system is working. If we want to change those features that we thought of as problems, then we have to be prepared for everything to change.

If we're wise, we also know how to keep that rapture; how to rekindle the belief that all is possible. Not because we believe in our power to change the whole world, but because the vision is beautiful and gives us the energy.

The end may be in sight, but today's journey is all I really have. Let me make the most of it.

*Every great mistake has a halfway moment, a split second
when it can be recalled and perhaps remedied.*
                                        —Pearl S. Buck

We make mistakes because we are human, we
are imperfect, we are frequently out of touch
with the rhythms of the moment. When our
minds are one place, either still trapped by the
past or in limbo due to fear of the future, we
fail to revere the experience of the present.
And only when we salute completely the moment do we respond accurately to its meaning.

Seldom is a mistake as important as we
allow it to be. Always we can rechart our steps;
never is a task completed without some modi-
fications along the way. Perhaps we'd do well
to consider all mistakes as simply modifica-
tions in the original plans. Corrections triggered by mistakes may well be responsible for
better outcomes. In fact, mistakes may be part
of the process necessary to keep our spiritual
program focused. Their role in our lives may
be of greater significance than we'd ever imag-
ined. However, we shouldn't dwell on the mistake but, rather, on the remedy.

*Today I'll have to modify my steps, probably
a few times. And that's to be expected.*

Courage is fear that has said its prayers.
—Anonymous

No one of us is always courageous. With trepidation we embark on many journeys. Fear is dispelled each time we rely on our inner strength and trust that our lives are in good hands.

Self-talk is powerful and will prepare us to meet whatever lies ahead today. Self-talk is like prayer and quiets our fears, making it possible to give our full attention to the events transpiring. Self-talk, when positive, cultivates a healthy self-image, one that offers security, even in the face of disaster. We all carry on a dialogue with ourselves much of the time. Taking charge of the messages—making sure they enhance our personal well-being—is an option always available to us.

No situation is more than we can handle. Whatever courage or strength is needed is as close as our willingness to go within, to commune with ourselves.

I must own my fears before I can let them go. Courage follows closely on their departing footsteps.

She walks around all day
quietly, but underneath it
she's electric angry energy inside a passive form.
The common woman is as common
as a thunderstorm.

—Judy Grahn

Many people spend their days in anger and aren't aware of it. The conditions of work and life make many of us angry; we feel powerless to change them, and our frustration angers us more.

The Serenity Prayer asks for "the serenity to accept the things I cannot change, the courage to change the things I can, and the wisdom to know the difference." If we examine our lives fearlessly, we may find many things that are in our power to change.

Since we cannot change, or do not choose to change some things, we'd do well to accept them, instead of spinning our wheels in unproductive anger or turning the anger in, against ourselves. And when we summon the courage to change the things we can, our lives will bless us.

Today I'll look at anger as something I've chosen, instead of something inevitable. Is it covering fear? How can I resolve it?

April 23

One often learns more from ten days of agony than from ten years of contentment.
—Merle Shain

Pain pushes us, sometimes gently, sometimes forcefully. It pushes us to make or accept changes in our lives. We do not always welcome change. Often the change even seems to intensify the pain for a spell. But in time we'll clearly see the need for the change.

The peaceful periods in our lives have their purpose, too. They give us time to rest, to grow accustomed to the changes, to nurture the "new self" that the changes made.

Accepting all experiences as necessary to our development removes the negativity we are likely to attach to these experiences. We might instead choose to celebrate those difficult times, recognizing their worth to our human potential.

A positive attitude today will enhance the value of every experience. The choice is open to me.

I have learned silence from the talkative; tolerance from the intolerant and kindness from the unkind. I should not be ungrateful to those teachers.

—Kahlil Gibran

Every situation we experience, every individual we encounter offers us valuable insights about living life more fully. We learn what we appreciate in people by confronting what disturbs us. We are certain to learn more about ourselves when we acknowledge that which displeases us in the experiences that enjoy our attention.

It's all too easy to label "of no value" experiences that, on the surface, bore us. We also discount persons whose life experiences are different than our own. It takes a decision followed by concentrated effort to recognize the value of every moment. Each one is serving us a lesson that deserves our full attention, and it's frequently true that the lessons most helpful are the ones least appreciated or understood in the present.

I can be certain that whatever situations disturb me today are also guaranteed to offer me unexpected growth.

April 25

[In the 16th century] one has only to consider the difficulties involved in feeding a baby if the mother's milk ran dry.
—Philippe Avies

Scientific progress has brought our society to the point where such a natural disaster as a milkless mother need have no consequences for her or her infant. Clean water, sewage disposal, immunization, and a widely available varied diet ensure relatively good health for millions. Sometimes this tempts us to look at the past as if it were another planet or the history of another species.

People had the same feelings four hundred years ago as we have today. Life was brutally hard; no families expected that all the children born would survive to maturity; people were old at 35 and often dead at 45. But they loved, feared, raged, and sought spiritual peace as we do.

Visiting old cemeteries is a moving experience, and an exercise for the imagination. Here is a man who buried three wives; here a family that lost four children in four years. We can reconstruct a different world in an hour or two and give ourselves an occasion for gratitude.

Imagining myself into the difficulties of the past can broaden my sympathies for the present.

It is more profitable to turn away thine eyes from such things as displease thee than to be a slave to contention.
—Thomas à Kempis

Focusing our attention incessantly on matters that disturb us, keeps us disturbed. And our obsession with our problems leaves no room for their solutions. However, we are only powerless in the face of difficulties if we choose to be. We are always free to search for the good which is lost in a tangled situation. We can be certain that our progress in life is equal to our capacity to let go of our problems and move ahead with the momentum of a positive attitude.

All too frequently, we fail to recognize opportunities for growth and success because we have chosen to be trapped by circumstances that are beyond our control. We may not realize this but we are never tied to problems. Solutions are always within our grasp. However, we must let go long enough to gain a responsible perspective on the situation.

Problems need not stifle my growth today.

All the strong things of her heart came out in her body,
that had been so tireless in serving generous emotions.
                                        —Willa Cather

We're always fascinated by beauty, and we see
it as the outward sign of goodness. For young
children, anything that brings pleasure is
good: soft fur, music, colored lights, candy.
What a disappointment to find that the soft
kitten has claws that scratch!

As we mature, our notions of beauty and
pleasure deepen and become more complex.
We see that beauty in people often is a reflection of their spiritual selves—and that physical
beauty is a little shallow and unsatisfying unless a generous spirit accompanies it.

That's what we call straightening out our
priorities: deciding or discovering that virtue
isn't boring, it's essential. Honesty, depend-
ability, and truth are what we look for in others and what we strive for in ourselves. They
wear better than clothes or cars.

There's a saying, "In middle age, we have
the faces we deserve." Everyone has seen the
wreckage that selfishness or dissipation can
leave on the faces of old beauties. When we
have strong, durable, compassionate spirits,
we will be good to look at.

Strength and tenderness are more beautiful
than high cheekbones or curling hair, and I
deserve them in my relationships.

A soft answer turneth away wrath but grievous words stir up anger.

—Book of Proverbs

Our treatment of others in the home, at work, or at play is our invitation for similar treatment. In fact, our every action, be it overt or covert, is noted by someone. We are always teaching someone how to treat us.

Anger is a seductive teacher. Unwanted tension, missed opportunities, stifled growth, are all we can expect if we're trapped by anger. Our chances for creative fulfillment will be unnoticed when our attention is sapped by anger. But we can change our basic response to life. All it takes is a decision.

Just as powerful as negative behavior is a positive, friendly approach to situations and persons. We can decide to love life. And we'll find that smiles invite smiles. Respect generates respect. A serene attitude lessens tension in others. Each of us is responsible for our own actions, and we each have the power to positively influence all experiences we share with others.

How I'm treated today will mirror how I'm treating others. Will I be proud?

April 29

I too am born and
grown to be this thing only;
to be Anna in the world.
                    —Anna Rydstedt-Dannstedt

In all the world there is no one like you or like me. Even identical twins are not wholly alike. The sum of genetic information, experience, learning, desire, and memory that makes up each individual is absolutely unique. At any given moment we represent that sum—and the next moment the sum is different.

It follows that each of us is best in the world at one thing—being ourselves. To let go of competition with others is to release within ourselves the creative energy to be the best we can. We need never stop growing; the task of developing our individuality lasts our whole life. Fortunately, it's an absorbing task, and one that each one of us happens to be uniquely suited for.

To be ourselves in the world is a glorious thing. We should stretch our spirits so that we inhabit our lives fully, and we will learn all we can.

Let this day be my teacher, and my mirror.

In nature there are neither rewards nor punishments— there are consequences.

—Robert G. Ingersoll

In life, as in nature, we experience the consequences of our actions. Some consequences benefit us in very positive ways. Others teach harsh lessons. But no action avoids having some effect on our lives and on the lives of other people, too. It is fortunate that each of us has personal power over our actions. Individually and collectively we are in control, every moment, of the actions that culminate in good or bad consequences for all humanity.

It is easy to overlook the ramifications of our haughty attitude toward a co-worker, or our temper tantrum because we thought a loved one let us down. We easily justify our treatment of others, and seldom take responsibility for the consequences we triggered. And yet our emotional maturity and our personal happiness are directly related to our commitment to behave in a responsible manner. We not only adversely affect others by our negative behavior, we hamper our personal progress, too.

My actions are far-reaching, as are their consequences. I will take care to make them positive today.

May

May 1

The body repeats the landscape. They are the source of each other and create each other.

       —Meridel Le Sueur

The beautiful correspondences that structure the world—from the five-pointed star in the core of the apple to the snail-shell spiral of our inner ear—can be a source of great comfort to us. When we feel most alone, most abandoned, and out of sorts, the simple forms of beauty can remind our eyes of the world's unity and our place within it.

Our path through the world is a part of it. We add our individual voices to the chord that is language, that is history. No matter how desperate we may feel, or how hopeless our lives may seem at times, the fact remains that loss and sorrow are a part of life, and the law of life is change. Unless we choose to cling to sorrow, it will flow through us. The next wave of feeling may bring us joy.

The hexagonal cells of the honeycomb recall the shapes of insects' eyes, snowflakes, geodesic domes. We fit into this grand design. We're here for a reason—for many reasons. Let us treat ourselves as gently as we try to treat the other parts of the delicate web of life.

I stand in a reciprocal relationship with the world, part of it as it is part of me.

Resolve to be thyself and know that he who finds himself loses his misery.

—Matthew Arnold

How confusing the issues in our lives can be when we try to accommodate all the views of the persons in our midst, persons who share few opinions in common. Agreeing with first one and then another is dizzying, and makes us suspect in the eyes of others. "Who is she really?" "What does he honestly believe?" We quickly become ill at ease in the company of those whose opinions we share only when it's convenient to do so.

We can be at peace when we've thoughtfully determined a course of action, and a world view that's compatible. Our attitudes, our opinions, and thus our responses to the currents of life will be consistent. When we develop integrity and strive to maintain it, rather than being in constant internal conflict because of our fluctuation, we discover a smoother passage over the bumps each of us can expect in life.

Today will be much less stressful if my actions reflect my inner self.

Our doubts are traitors,
And make us lose the good we oft might win
By fearing to attempt.
                    —William Shakespeare

Our own doubts are our greatest barriers in any endeavors. We are only free and able to accomplish what we think we can. When doubt arises, defeat is not far behind. However, that principle is just as strong in reverse. When we believe in ourselves, nothing can hold us back. Our accomplishments are many when we've developed the habit of self-assurance.

We must take personal responsibility for our beliefs, whether they be positive or negative. No one else is capable of putting thoughts in our minds. We have chosen those that are there. Far better that we coach our minds along positive paths. Only they can lead to the accomplishments that will give us satisfaction, today and every day.

We can anticipate our victories with excitement in this life. They will reflect what we've coached ourselves to attempt.

What I feel myself today will very much influence my achievement.

The most prophetic utterances have emanated from the most poetical minds.

—William F. R. Stanley

What we call poetry is a capacity to use language so freely, so beautifully, and with so much imagination that it transforms ordinary words. What we call prophecy is the ability to see through the complex machinery of the present into the true nature of events. Both the poet and the prophet seem to be touched with magic—with more than human powers.

They tear aside the veil of ordinary reality. Both reveal a vision more intense than ours. Yet we can learn from poets and prophets, if we wish. Their vision is available to us.

All we need is humility and a willingness to let our minds play freely. Great prophets and poets speak to our human condition. Their vision can challenge or console us, if we consult them.

Truth is truth; I can recognize it where I find it.

May 5

He that knew all that learning ever writ
Knew only this—that he knew nothing yet.
                                        —Aphra Behn

It's true that the more information we have about the world, the more clearly we see the shape of what we don't know. It's also true that we don't need to learn anything at all in order to deal fairly with others and to walk gently in the world.

The wisdom that we need is inside us. Before our schooling teaches us to forget it, we know instinctively how to treat others because we know how we wish others to treat us, and we know that all people are one.

This primitive knowledge mustn't be buried under the classifications and analyses we pick up along the way. We can, if we try, de-school ourselves to the point where we can listen to our spirits, trust our bodies, and revere the world for the seamless whole it is.

If I cherish my original wisdom, then learning can help me to be comfortable in my ignorance.

Fear is only an illusion. It is the illusion that creates the feeling of separateness—the false sense of isolation that exists only in your imagination.
                                    —Jeraldine Saunders

We are only alone in our minds. In reality, we are each contributing and necessary parts offering completion to the wholeness of the universe. Our very existence guarantees our equality, which, when fully understood, eases our fears. We have no reason to fear one another's presence, or to fear new situations when we realize that all of us are on equal footing. No one's talents are of greater value than our own, and each of us is talented in ways exactly appropriate to our circumstances.

Freedom from fear is a decision we can choose to make at any time. We can simply give it up and replace it with our understanding of equality with all persons. Taking responsibility for our fear, or our freedom from it, is the first step to a perspective promising healthier emotional development.

If I am fearful today it's because I've forgotten the reality of my existence. I am equal to all the people in my world, and we are necessary to one another.

May 7

There is no cardinal who does not aspire to the papacy.
                                        —Stendahl

When we think of it, there is something truly remarkable in the fact that practically all human beings want to be better than they are. What a hopeful reading of the human race—four billion people, all eager to improve themselves!

For many of the humans on earth, self-improvement has an economic basis—to be able to eat two or three times each day, perhaps, rather than once. We are fortunate to be able to understand improvement in a moral and spiritual sense. Increased income or possessions cannot truly augment us; our real growth is inward.

However we understand our spiritual selves, most of us agree on how to foster them: through peace, silence, and beauty, in meditation, and in what some of us call prayer. Just as every bud aspires to be a flower, and as the flower holds the secret of the fruit, so we enfold the beauty of our spirits. If we nourish the spirit, we can grow to be our better selves. If we allow nothing to hamper its growth, our spirit will unfold.

I shall set my eyes on the clear path toward my spiritual unfolding.

Our true age can be determined by the ways in which we allow ourselves to play.

—Louis Walsh

Too few of us laugh as heartily as we might. We often fail to see the humorous side of our lives. We respond gravely to most situations, certain that a serious perspective is called for. We are unaware, it seems, that we're charged only with living responsibly. Never are we asked to be solely serious.

Any situation is easier to handle if our response is lighthearted. Laughter and playfulness ease the tensions inherent in certain circumstances. Taking life less seriously doesn't mean living less responsibly. Rather, it means freeing ourselves from the negative forces that may well encumber the circumstances facing us presently.

It's difficult even to recall what tripped me last week, and this fact alone should bring relief while I'm looking at today's potential hazards.

May 9

Breaking through the foreground which is the Playboys'
Playground means letting out the bunnies, the bitches, the
beavers, the squirrels, the chicks, the pussycats, the cows, the
nags, the foxy ladies, the old bats and biddies so that they
can at last begin naming themselves.

—Mary Daly

Racial and sexual stereotyping, casual put-downs that consign another person to non-human status, is so demeaning that it's hard to believe the speaker really means it. We've become so habituated to the put-down that it's hard to be aware of how disrespectful this can be, to ourselves as well as others.

This competitive attitude keeps us jockeying for position, leads us constantly to measure where we stand, and assumes that there's only a limited amount of rightness in the world.

We're both all right, and if we're going to have a relationship that lets us be self-respectful as well as respectful of one another, we'll act as if we're both all right. We won't call one another chicks, pigs, big apes, or foxes. We won't call each other by our body parts or our ethnic groups, either; we'll recognize each other's full and individual humanity.

I will live today in honor of my name, and thus
honor others.

*There are as many ways to live and grow as there are peo-
ple. Our own ways are the only ways that should matter
to us.*

—Evelyn Mandel

Letting other people grow, develop, live their
own experiences as they must takes courage
and acceptance of the knowledge that our responsibility in this life is to our own healthy
development—not to controlling someone
else's.

It's not easy to let go of someone with whom
we want to share a particular path in life; however, no two of us are destined for exactly the
same lessons today or any day. We must each
find our own way and develop those opportunities we meet that are certain to enhance the
lessons our souls have been created for.

Our need to control someone else generally results from our own insecurities about
life's meaning. Because we lack understanding
of our own personal worth, we look for it in
someone else's devotion to us—a devotion
that, in time, we squeeze the life from.

We cannot control another's behavior, and
yet we try. And the more we try the greater
the barriers between us become. Trust is all we
finally have that each of us is progressing, according to our own pace, in rightful company.
We cannot force what is not meant to be.

*My own pace and direction are all that I need
to be concerned with today.*

The distance doesn't matter; only the first step is difficult.
                                        —Mme. du Deffand

Life continually presents us with opportunities
for achieving what we desire. "Only the first
step is difficult." Each time we sense the possibility of a new direction in our lives, we are
being given a chance to grow.

Sometimes the first step is a big one; sometimes we start to take it almost without notic-
ing: a dream, a book, a conversation.
Sometimes growth may come from not taking
what looks like an opportunity. Whatever
choice we make we can be challenged to grow.

"The distance doesn't matter." Our road
has many branching paths. What we work and
pray for is the ability to see those paths clearly,
and the strength to take a difficult first step.

Today my first step may be surrender.

Hope is a good breakfast, but it is a bad supper.
—Francis Bacon

Each day we hope for accomplishment and satisfaction, and we'll achieve these when we scale our hopes to our real capacities. There's no more satisfying feeling than finishing a project we've set up ourselves, tailored to our abilities, and worked at with patience and care. Our lives can be filled with such successes.

Learning to live means learning to keep ourselves in the present. This day is all we really have to work with. Of course, today will be influenced by what has already happened; and its influence will extend to tomorrow, next week, and beyond. But all we can make or do lies here, within this window of space and time.

May my supper be contentment. I'll breakfast on hope again tomorrow.

To keep your character intact you cannot stoop to filthy acts.
It makes it easier to stoop the next time.
> —Katherine Hepburn

Good habits are as easily formed as bad ones. It's quite likely that most of our daily activities are routine. With little need for forethought, we make our necessary motions every day. And if we've behaved toward others in disrespectful ways on many occasions, we may thoughtlessly repeat those acts today.

Yet we should be grateful that we are in full control of all actions we choose to take. No one else has power over our behavior. No one else can push us into actions for which we'll feel shame or remorse.

Responsibility for who we are, in all respects, is our birthright. Perhaps we don't always rejoice over this fact. And yet, it is the one absolute that guarantees we each have the power to become who we wish to become.

I'm creating behavior patterns today. Will they make me proud?

*However much we guard against it, we tend to shape
ourselves in the image others have of us.*
                                        —Eric Hoffer

Our sense of how someone else perceives us
is a compelling influence in our lives. At such
times we've often chosen not to rely on our
personal power, which can forge the posture
we want to present to others. We must put
forth the effort, however. Passively letting
others decide who we are gives us who we
deserve!

We are not powerless in any situation. It's
true that we cannot control others, but the reverse is likewise true. Unfortunately, too often
we let another individual decide our worth,
our capabilities, our very personality. Domi-
neering parents may have done it in the past.
A hateful boss or a too-critical spouse may do
it presently. We are always responsible for our
participation in someone else's underestima-
tion of us. We are who we want to be. The
question we must answer is, why do we choose
to satisfy someone's negative image?

*Self-talk will help me maintain the self-image
I choose today. I will accept personal responsibility.*

A man is rich in proportion to the number of things he can afford to let alone.

—Henry David Thoreau

Conscious, careful selection of those activities, situations, or people to whom we'll devote attention is all that separates centered, serene people from harried men and women. All of us are bombarded by myriad requests for some form of personal involvement. The temptation is great to attend to first one thing and then another, passively and superficially. However, our lives are enriched only when we commit ourselves to a deeper level of involvement, and to the few, rather than the many.

The talent given each of us shines forth if it's been nurtured, coddled, encouraged. We must become immersed enough in a project or an experience to lose self-conscious reservations if we're to discover the real weight of our talent. We know ourselves fully only when we're able to let the talent within define the posture without.

I can't be all things to all people today if I'm to be the person I need to be for me.

I am determined to maintain the perpendicular position.
                                        —Lucy Stone

Perpendicular lines make right angles; they make possible extensions of both height and breadth. Right angles are weight-bearing. We speak of asserting something "squarely," making perpendiculars.

People who speak their minds freely and assert their individuality feel perpendicular; the corners they create, by their points of view, are sturdy and open. Others can use them to build structures on.

It's important to claim the perpendicular, even though we may feel pressured into curved or parallel positions. If we're centered in ourselves, others won't throw us off balance. Each of us needs to find our own center so that we can occupy our own place. Others will recognize us. Together we'll build high and wide.

My remotest ancestors dared to point their spines upright. I'll carry on the project they began.

Who cannot give good counsel? 'Tis cheap it costs them nothing.

—Robert Burton

Other people's problems are so easy to solve. Isn't it amazing how much better we are at their lives than our own? Of course, other people's lives don't hook us emotionally, by means of love or guilt or precious delusions. We can look at them wisely, with detachment.

Detachment is the key to solving our own problems, too, except that the detached intelligence may see a solution we're unwilling to use—especially if it means changing our behavior. Then we may feel despair. We're stuck, between the rock of our intelligence and the hard place of our reluctance to change.

Whether we stay stuck depends on us. We can choose to live as hybrids, a little wise, a little infantile; a little happy, a little miserable. Or we can risk change and growth. Within us is the knowledge and power to get what we want, if we'll believe in ourselves.

My problems are like other people's. Whether I solve them or not is up to me.

Memory is the power to gather roses in winter.
—Anonymous

What a marvelous capacity we each have to capture and savor the bliss of past moments. They serve to comfort us while we're enduring the pain of the present. However, it's this present experience that has called us to attention. Within its context we'll be challenged to tackle the lessons for which past memories have prepared us.

Notwithstanding the comfort of the past, we'd do well not to hang on to past memories unrelentingly. Only by flowing with the present and absorbing how these events punctuate our lives, are we grasping the full experience our lives offer. There are too many people who live half-lives, and thus find half-joys because they fail to give up the past for the fuller measure that is offered in the present.

Fortunately, we are blessed with the power to live here and now, or in the past, if we so choose. Freedom of choice is the special gift of the human condition.

I'll appreciate my gift of choice today and linger in the past only as it benefits the better part of the present.

Everything's got a moral, if you can only find it.
                                        —Lewis Carroll

To say that life is full of meaning is not to say that meaning is fixed or magical. Signs come to us from within, not from outside; the morals we can draw from the little dramas in our lives have to do with our own growth.

We can learn from negative experiences as well as positive ones, and we need to applaud our own progress (it's likely no one else will). Only we can know how far we have travelled when we overcome a fear of speaking in public, or joining a volunteer telephone campaign. Or perhaps we've learned to say "no" to the constant demands others make of us; we're the only ones who recognize that advance, and we deserve to congratulate ourselves for it.

Finding the morals in daily events can be an adventure. It's good to take stock periodically; it helps us to see what progress we've made and to scale our expectations to the real pace of our growth.

Today I'll hold a private viewing of some of my recent successes; I'll be my own best audience.

Our deeds still travel with us from afar,
And what we have been makes us what we are.
— George Eliot

Changing cities, countries, jobs, or partners
can't change what we are; that change only
comes from within us, from deep searching
and redirection of our values and behaviors.
Yet many of us blithely hope that a physical
move will work a spiritual change. Still others
trust in the delusion that a new relationship
can transform the self that has developed
slowly over our whole lives.

If we like ourselves pretty well, we can acknowledge our past. We'll own the choices we
made at this or that juncture, and we can see
the results. But if we're dissatisfied with how
we're doing, if we feel the need to change our
lives, we must recognize that hard work will
be involved, hard choices and some pain.

Feeling the need is usually painful in itself.
Often it means we're ready for those hard
choices, and much of the work is already going
on, deep within. Only a little more spiritual
housecleaning, absolute honesty about our
motives, and we may accomplish what we seek
to change.

Wherever I am, in the twisting road of my life,
is where I'm meant to be.

Obstinacy in a bad cause is but constancy in a good.
—Sir Thomas Browne

Faults, when they're closely examined, often turn out to be the other end of virtues. Carelessness in one situation might be generosity in another; secretiveness might turn out to be an extension of tact. In most of us, positive and negative attributes are related to one another like positive and negative photographic prints. The way we see the image depends on the situation and the light.

Quickness to anger can also mean quickness to forgive, to understand, or to move quickly in emergencies. A slow reaction time may go along with thoughtful caution. Understanding of ourselves will grow when we come to see ourselves along a continuum, where the traits that hold us back in one situation may be advantages in another. As we understand ourselves, we learn to love ourselves better, as we deserve.

Today I will look at my behavior to see whether a fault I don't like about myself might not be the other end of an asset.

The ego is a self-justifying historian which seeks only that information that agrees with it, rewrites history when it needs to, and does not even see the evidence that threatens it.
—Anthony G. Greenwald

One of the larger struggles facing us is relinquishing the need to be right always. Only when we've given up the struggle do we understand that the battle is finally won. We come to see nonresistance as the quintessence of the power play. However, our need to be right is the point of real concern, and in order to let go of this need, clarity regarding the human condition is in order.

Few of us are sure of our worth, our necessity to the better functioning of the human universe. We falter and fear our mistakes, certain that they will enlighten our fellow travelers about our inadequacies. And so we bully others, covertly or with great poise, into accepting our viewpoints. We believe that ideas shared by others are more valuable, and thus our own value is assured. No one is served by the exercises in truth.

Might the time finally come when I will understand that my individual existence is all the proof I need that I am right—without the struggle? I can practice this belief today.

May 23

"Living in the forest" would mean sinking into one's innermost nature and finding out what it feels like.
                    —Marie-Louise von Frantz

Our innermost nature—that fearsome place where our dreams dwell—what would we find there? Crude passions, lust, rage, and selfishness, or a void, a sadness without end? Many people do fear themselves, and their personalities are built on a shaky foundation of mistrust.

These are people who don't seem to confront their feelings very successfully. They may have trouble acknowledging resentments or desires, out of some sense that they ought to be above such human impulses. Unfortunately, it is often the very people who have such unrealistic expectations of themselves who surprise everyone with sudden violence. "They were such nice quiet people," everyone says, after the scandalous divorce or the suicide.

Getting to know our inner geography, our own pattern of needs and fears, is never dangerous. The danger lies in refusing to know. We can't build solid self-confidence on ignorance and mistrust of ourselves; only by loving ourselves and acknowledging our kinship with needy, fearful humanity can we grow as individuals.

My roots in the forest will keep my head out of the clouds.

Toleration is the greatest gift of the mind.
> —Helen Keller

With immeasurable ease we are able to pass through difficult times if we are tolerant of the people and circumstances that are beyond our control. Toleration is an acquired trait, but one that's cherished once it's securely developed.

Toleration comes more easily when the real nature of our existence is understood. Our lives are purposeful; however, no two lives share exactly the same goals or path. Each of us is fulfilling a destiny that's designed only for ourselves; others' activities or manners will be fitting only to them. Peace of mind is our due, but it will elude us if we're ever trapped by our desire to direct another's steps.

Freedom to live the day fully accompanies a tolerant attitude. Precious moments that could enhance personal development need never be wasted on fantasies of controlling others—fantasies that can never become realities.

My achievements today can be many if I'm not wasting precious moments anguishing over persons I can't control.

. . . my grief was too deeply rooted to be cured with words.
                                        —Orinda

We give enormous power to words in our culture. Most of us have given words the power to hurt us, at times, and we have also given them the power to heal. Many of us say prayers that have a special meaning, invoking deep comfort and putting us in touch with our spiritual essence.

Life deals wounds that can't be healed even by these precious soothing words. For many of us there will be times when all our strength is needed simply to endure, to live from one moment to the next. At such times, silence has more power than words. We're fortunate if we've developed our capacity to meditate to empty ourselves, and seek the still point.

The wounded spirit shrinks from words. They can never say all we mean, and words always carry the world with them. We must cultivate the serenity that lies beyond words. It has a nourishing power.

Today I shall remember that silence can heal the wounded spirit.

*. . . the absence of love in our lives is what makes them
seem raw and unfinished.*

—Ingrid Bengis

Love expressed softens the harsh cutting edge
of any experience. Whether we're the recipi-
ents of love or the givers, we still share in the
promised rewards, the greatest of which is the
knowledge that we belong, that others know
us. We know we're not alone when we feel another's love, and when we have someone to
give love to.

Independence and self-reliance are worthy
attributes, and may prepare any one of us for
survival in hard times. However, if they inter-
fere with our awareness of and praise for the
interdependent nature of the world, we'll discover that our personal survival is at stake.
Our emotional, intellectual, and physical development is enhanced by our involvement
with others.

The alienation any of us feels at this moment can be quickly dispelled if we'd but offer
the hand of love and willingly receive it in
turn. Our lives are rich and fulfilling in proportion to the love exchanged among us.

*I will let someone else know I love them today
and cherish the good feeling it gives me.*

It is impossible that anything should be produced if there were nothing existing before.

—Aristotle

Everything comes from something. All the organic compounds in our world come from four elements: carbon, hydrogen, oxygen, and nitrogen. From these simple ingredients have developed the marvelous chains of self-replicating proteins that fill the planet with jungles, gardens, farms, the swarming life of the sea, and four billion people.

Each of us contains all human possibilities within ourselves. Nothing that we do comes from nowhere; we all have the capacity for great goodness as well as great selfishness and blindness. The choice, at every moment, is ours. What will we use, out of our formidable repertoire of responses?

Most of us have a pattern of response that we are comfortable with. Our habitual behavior saves us from the discomfort of always having to make a choice. But in exchange for comfort, we give up a little bit of our spontaneity. Every once in a while, it's good for us to become aware of what our habits are, and what determines our usual behavior.

Today I'll take myself off automatic pilot and navigate the whole course in person.

Happiness is a by-product of an effort to make someone else happy.

—Gretta Brooker Palmer

Self-centeredness aggravates the natural flow of circumstances surrounding us; too much attention on ourselves distorts whatever might be troubling us. However, focusing on others' needs diminishes what we'd perceived as our own pressing need. This is a simple principle we might all consider adopting.

None of us is free of problems. That's one of life's givens. Through their resolution we grow and ready ourselves for the next group of challenges. Each group survived enables us to offer better assistance to someone else who will confront a similar problem. Perhaps we'd do well to see all our problems as preparation for guiding someone who will come into our life. Helping someone else is certain to lift spirits and foster happiness, but the unexpected reward is that the helper reaps even greater benefits than the one helped.

My happiness is guaranteed if I help someone else find it today.

People noticed and respected families that included many old people, knowing that in those families must be industrious, wise, and spiritual women who gathered good foods, prepared meats properly, and made daily offerings and prayers to the spirits.

—Mary Louise Defender

Until the recent past, the health of her extended family was a woman's responsibility. Perhaps the American Indians were unusually wise in appreciating the health-giving qualities of both good nutrition and spiritual practice. We sometimes forget how important a tranquil spirit is to our overall health.

Health, as a positive quality, expresses how well we integrate with the world. It's measured by the success of our detachment from those things we can do nothing about, as well as by our engagement with those things we can. A healthy organism cooperates with natural processes and throws off insults.

More and more, we are taking responsibility for our own health. If we live to a ripe old age, it won't necessarily be because of our daughters-in-law or our nieces, but because we've learned to respect the balance of the body and spirit. "Daily offerings and prayer," that is, daily meditation and spiritual cleansing, is something we can all incorporate into our lives. Whatever our life span, it will be richer and happier if we nourish our spirit along with our bodies.

Many sources of wisdom are available to me, and the strong voice of the spirit sounds in them all.

*To live in dialogue with another is to live twice. Joys are
doubled by exchange and burdens are cut in half.*
—Wishart

We live in one another's company for a reason.
The talents any one of us is gifted with are
most pleasurable when used to benefit many.
And each of us is talented in ways unique and
yet burdensome if not shared.

Our personal growth and development are
dependent in part on the contributions made
by those we're in company with. We live better because of others' presence and talented
contributions to situations affecting us all.
Likewise, others are equally benefitted by our
positive involvement in their lives.

We need one another to diffuse the pain
and sorrow in our lives. Sharing lessens the
weight on a single pair of shoulders. Sharing
also reminds us that none of us is burdened in
ways unfamiliar to others. Laughing together
multiplies our appreciation of someone else's
involvement in our lives. Every aspect of life
promises more meaning when shared openly
with another. We could even say that no event
is really integrated into a life if experienced in
isolation.

*I'll find meaning today in the company of
others.*

"Yes," I answered you last night,
"No," this morning, sir, I say.
Colours seen by candle light
Will not look the same by day.
    —Elizabeth Barrett Browning

Circumstances alter cases. We all know that important decisions require time and preparation, yet many of us make them impulsively or on inadequate information.

When was the last time we made a mistake in judgment and admitted it? Whether it has to do with the color of our walls or the terms of a contract or the person we said we'd marry, admitting that we've changed our minds is far more honorable than going through with a wrong decision.

There used to be a saying, "It's a woman's prerogative to change her mind." It's everyone's prerogative, because nobody's perfect. We are all influenced "by candle light." To be too proud or inflexible to alter a decision, even when we've changed our minds, is a good way to set ourselves up for misery.

Joining the human race is much preferable to fighting it. I will be human enough today to admit my mistakes, and free enough to change my mind.

June

The tail of the kite, it is true, seems to negate the kite's function: it weights down something made to rise . . .
　　　　　　　　　　　—Cleanth Brooks

Without its tail, the kite would fly off in the lightest breeze. The tail serves as a rudder, to steady the kite and allow it to be directed. Every force needs a counter-force to channel it effectively.

Ancient philosophers looked on the body as ballast for the mind. Without our physical anchor, they thought, our desires, our imaginations, our ideas would run away with us and the world would go to wrack and ruin.

Our minds and our bodies aren't two different things. They're made of the same stuff. They make up one being. We can never say where one leaves off and the other begins, nor can we say that one weighs down the other.

We can say, though, that we contain within ourselves all sorts of contradictions, checks, and counter-forces. This makes life interesting. Looked at positively, it means that we can understand any human possibility because we contain them all.

Contradictions only bother me before I can see them as parts of a larger whole.

Our grand business is not to see what lies dimly at a distance, but to do what lies clearly at hand.
—Thomas Carlyle

First things first. How much more simply life could evolve if we'd but focus our attention on the obvious situation confronting us, looking always for our direction from within the situation's elements.

How little point there is in worrying about what may come, and yet we expend incalculable amounts of energy in just such activity. What lies before us is all there really is in our lives—today. Nothing confronts us without purpose. Whatever the situation, it has called us forth to act. Our action will benefit us if we choose to transcend the ego that invites our worry, our smallness in thought and behavior.

Today stands before me, awaiting my involvement. I will go peacefully, addressing only those situations that invite my attention, and I will give it, fully.

June 3

Maybe if I listen closely to the rocks
Next time, I'll hear something, if not
A word, perhaps the faint beginning of a syllable.
                              —Phoebe Hanson

Everything in the world has something to say
to us: rocks, garbage, even our disappoint-
ments and failures. For everything belongs to
the vast, pulsating pattern that is the earth.
Nothing that exists does not belong; if we find
this or that piece of the pattern troublesome,
it's because we haven't perceived its contribution to the whole.

Sometimes, when we're feeling down on
ourselves, nothing seems to fit. What we're
really feeling is isolated and sorry for ourselves—"out of sorts," that is, unmatched.
Why do we do this to ourselves—pretend
we're different, pretend that no one can understand us? It's a childish game, really; we're
surrounded by pattern pieces that we match
like lock and key, even the rocks by the cabin
door.

I will listen closely. Who knows? I might hear
something I need to learn.

No person in the world ever attempted to wrong another without being injured in return—some way, somehow, sometime.

—William George Jordan

Whatever our actions today, they will repay us in kind. Our choices will be many, as will our opportunities. Kindness fosters kindness. Respect elicits respect. A positive attitude clears the way for smooth sailing.

We create the world we find by our every action. No thought escapes the ripple effect. Each response we make to another, or to a situation, sets in motion a new wave of activity that will find its way back to us, in time.

To each moment we owe attention, and we have total power regarding the form and the manner of our attention. We can be certain that whatever confronts us today has its roots in our own past action.

I can be certain that to invite positive opportunities in my tomorrows means meeting those of today with kindness of spirit.

June 5

Anyone can blame; it takes a specialist to praise.
                    —Konstantin Stanislavski

True praise is a form of love. Mystics and saints have seen the whole living, breathing world as a hymn of praise to the Creator Spirit. This spiritual vision implies that praise is both a natural act and an art; simply being can be a form of praise, and so can the most intricate skill.

When we praise another insincerely, we are often concealing other utterances—perhaps jealousy or fear. When was the last time we spoke praise with all our heart?

Blame is easy because we all know what it is to fail. And if we feel blameworthy ourselves, we like to enlist company, to point out others' failings. Why should we be so grudging of praise? Praise doesn't diminish us; to the contrary, it augments our spirit. We might seek out occasions for praise as a way of expanding our lives.

I will do what I can to become a specialist of praise.

Rudeness is a weak person's attempt at strength.
　　　　　　　　　—J. Matthew Casey

How others treat us indicates the self-assurance
attained by those persons. Confident, content,
self-respecting people are ably respectful of
others. We often doubt our ability, either physical or intellectual, because someone has heaped
criticism upon us.

　　The converse is likewise true. How we treat
others at any time clearly reveals our personal
contentment. We are not powerless over our
reactions, even to pressing situations or pushy
personalities. We can decide to behave admir-
ably, which in turn nurtures all personalities
and soothes every situation.

　　The adage, "we teach others how to treat
us," is a wise reminder when we contemplate
our actions and reactions.

*My behavior today is an open invitation to oth-
ers for treatment in kind. I will find responses
that are complementary to my own.*

June 7

Life is no argument. The conditions of life might include error.

—Friedrich Nietzsche

We've all known people to whom it was terribly important that they always be right. Perhaps some of us *are* those people, at least part of the time. Life under these conditions is an unrelenting struggle against sloppy thinking, dirt, carelessness, and the general slipshod stupidity of the rest of the world.

When we think this way, it is well to wonder how it is that we are right, while everyone else is wrong. We may find that our behavior is based not on rational thinking but on fear—the fear that if we relinquish control even for a moment, we'll fall into chaos.

How sad to be held hostage by such fears! The chaos we imagine at these times is no more real than the order we struggle to impose. What we need is self-acceptance—the humble but joyous recognition that we are human, just like everyone else, and that human beings might include error in their lives.

Perfection is an ideal, not a real phenomenon. Only by accepting my imperfection can I become fully human.

Doubt indulged soon becomes doubt realized.
—Frances Ridley Havergal

Self-confidence is not a given in our lives. It must be developed, often painstakingly, one task,.one account, one deadline at a time. And each day that we court indecision and doubt, we erode not only this development in process but the level of self-confidence that had already been attained.

There is very little in our lives that we have full control over. We can affect the outcome of a situation. The dynamics of a relationship reflect our input. But in most instances of our lives, we offer only a contribution. We do not have the power to totally control the outcome. However, in one area we do have full power. That area is attitude. And the attitude expressed on any occasion will profoundly affect the dynamics of the situation.

A confident posture in one instance makes easier the same posture in instances thereafter. Likewise, doubt breeds itself. The attitude we choose to express teaches others what to expect from us.

What posture will I assume today? The one I choose will directly affect all outcomes. I can move forward with assurance.

June 9

The solution to my life occurred to me one evening while I was ironing a shirt.

—Alice Munro

We all receive flashes of illumination, messages like shafts of lightning from one part of our brain to another. *This is the answer! This is the meaning of life!* Mathematicians tell stories of equations solved in a dream; we cling to the notion that an apple beaned Isaac Newton.

We all experience moments that seem like the brilliant knitting together of our fortunes. At such a moment, we are happy. We wish this could last forever. But the moment, like the illuminating flash, fades in intensity and is gone. The next moment holds something new.

What we may not remember is that these revelations and these moments of joy are prepared for, day by day. The slow building up of ordinary acts and thoughts prepares us for the flash of blinding clarity. The solution to our lives isn't a meteor; it's a mosaic, made up of many ordinary acts and choices, plans and reflections. And oh, how sweet the flashes, when they come!

Because I am the source of the questions, I really do know all the answers.

The worst sin towards our fellow creatures is not to hate them, but to be indifferent to them; that's the essence of inhumanity.

—George Bernard Shaw

The greatest gift we can give is rapt attention to one another's existence. Of one thing we can be certain: we each are in this world by design. Further, we are in one another's daily travels by invitation. We share a destiny, and our understanding and joy will be proportionate to our sincere attention to those we're obviously accompanying.

No opportunity for an exchange of words, simple gestures, quiet thoughts should be discounted or denied. Each moment of our lives offers us the necessary experiences for our full potential. We need one another's presence, contributions, even tribulations in order to move forward together as well as individually.

I go forth today alone and yet in good company. Everyone here in my life now is part of my destiny. Our trip is planned for today.

The mind is a baby giant who, more provident in the cradle than he knows, has hurled his paths in life all round ahead of him, like playthings. . . .

—Robert Frost

Sometimes we are bewildered by the options open to us. We feel we have no way of knowing which course would be best. But when we reflect calmly on our choices, we usually find very few that are realistic, that are in tune with our personalities and consonant with the rest of our lives.

It sometimes seems that a choice made, or an option dropped, when we are very young, can determine our whole lives. This is probably an illusion. Perhaps we believe that our fate was forever altered by missing a train ten years ago. Late at night, we might talk wistfully of what might have been, "If only I'd caught that train!"

Most likely, though, our lives would have turned out pretty much the same. What happens to us, and what we choose, seem to follow the same pattern—a pattern that is true for each one of us. We've marked out our paths, whether we're fully aware of them or not.

Sometimes I am indecisive because I desire to remain open to life's choices. Today I will act freely and strengthen that freedom by making responsible decisions.

Two may talk together under the same roof for many years, yet never really meet.

—Mary Catherwood

Conversation does not always assure, or even imply, self-revelation. Trading words is easily, frequently, and safely done; however, it doesn't introduce us to the one-another that resides within. Knowing one another can only be fostered by soul-baring.

Each of us needs to be wholly known by another. Only then, in the act of total self-disclosure, do we honestly confront ourselves. We learn in the process that our fears and our shame about our secret selves are far greater than is warranted. Silence about the "me" within distracts our perspective. Meeting another person fully reveals to both a new reality about life.

We cheat ourselves of the real pleasure in living when we hold ourselves back from someone close. Tearing down the barriers that separate us is exhilarating. Only when those barriers are down do we experience the full measure of the moment.

I will have a chance today to be whole and open with someone close. I'm guaranteed a reward when I take this opportunity.

June 13

Memories, like olives, are an acquired taste.
                    —Max Beerbohm

We've all learned to like different things as we've grown: different flavors, different colors, different music. There's no such thing as just naturally liking hockey or jazz; even if we're barely aware of doing so, we had to discipline ourselves to find the pattern of rewards in the game or the music.

It's no accident that the greater the effort we expend on acquiring a new taste, usually the greater the pleasure it gives us. Bridge is more fun than gin rummy; Bach wears better than Mantovani. It's true for other behaviors as well; the more of ourselves we invest, the greater the rewards.

This is nowhere so true as in relationships— the more we put in, the more we receive. A truly high quality of personal relationships is something we all deserve and too few of us get. We may settle for less than we deserve out of doubt or pity or the sneaking feeling that perhaps we don't deserve the best, after all.

The first and most important element is us— our own investment, the honesty and openness we bring to others, and the trust we are willing to bestow. Quality attracts quality; if we have trouble with our relationships, we'd do well to reevaluate the tastes we've acquired.

I'll look at my part; the only person I'm responsible for is me.

*There's a period of life when we swallow a knowledge of
ourselves and it becomes either good or sour inside.*
　　　　　　　　　　　　　　　　—Pearl Bailey

None of us is all good or all bad. Each of us
takes pride in some of our actions and suffers
shame for others. To be human guarantees up-
heavals; we are assured of shortcomings, and
we can count on glad tidings too. Taking all of
life's ebb and flow, smoothed by our own personal responses, leads us to a mellow maturity.

　Self-acceptance is mandatory if we are ever
to experience the sweetness of serenity. This
acceptance must be whole and unconditional,
not selective. We are who we know how to be
at the moment, nothing more. But we are in a
continual state of becoming. Whatever we've
said, thought, or done combines in untold
ways to enrich our experiences and the lives of
those we touch. Let's not be soured by the self
of the past, of yesterday even. Humbly accepting that portion of the whole will sweeten the
rest.

*I can avoid personal shame today if I think and
feel before acting or reacting.*

At Oran, as elsewhere, for lack of time and thinking, people have to love one another without knowing much about it.

—Albert Camus

What is time for? How often we say, "I don't have the time for—" meaning our marriages, our friends, our children, our hobbies, our parents, ourselves. Just what is important, anyway?

Some people seem to do everything in the margins of their lives, without thinking or knowing much about it. They go to school, get married, have children, get divorced, experience losses, get jobs, all rather offhandedly. Their attention always seems to be somewhere else.

All of us are preoccupied sometimes. And sometimes, in the middle of our lives, the preoccupation clears. "I woke up this morning and took a long look at my life. What have I gotten myself into!" Suddenly, somehow, our full attention is turned on the matter at hand. Suddenly, we have time to think. What's revealed then is the pattern of our lives. Did we make choices at random, irresponsibly? Now that we can see, are there parts to do over?

I'll endeavor to write my life story in the center of the page, not in the margins.

Hold fast to dreams for if dreams die,
life is a broken-winged bird that cannot fly.
                                        —Langston Hughes

Our dreams are our invitations to perform the
dance we've been gifted with. Dreams are full
of purpose. They mean to inspire us, acting as
markers along the paths to our destination.
Had we no dreams, we'd quickly lose the will
to live.

The twenty-four hours ahead will be filled
with dreams as well as actions. The actions we
take today are no doubt inspired by yesterday's
or last week's dreams. Dreams help us to image
that which our souls desire us to do. This im-
agery is powerful, helping us to be prepared
for any situation that requests our involvement.

Through our dreams we feel the pull of the
inner self—that center we each have which
knows our needs, our talents, our proper course
and destination. We need to nurture the tie to
the inner self; we can be grateful for our
dreams.

My lifeline to tomorrow is through today's
dream. I will respect its call.

The desire to believe the best of people is a prerequisite for intercourse with strangers; suspicion is reserved for friends.
— Mary McCarthy

How often we find ourselves treating our acquaintances with exquisite courtesy, while our friends and loved ones get our yawns, our sulks, our tantrums. We may pride ourselves on treating everyone alike, but most of us lapse into rudeness with our intimates. "It doesn't matter," we say. "They know me."

If someone doesn't know us, we behave with generosity. Why? To convince the stranger that we are nicer than we really are? Which is the ideal person, the one who is courteous to strangers, or the one who is rude to friends?

Mistrust of ourselves is the basis of these false values. Most of us fear, at one time or another, that we won't be liked, loved, or respected for ourselves alone. So we try to appear different, usually better. Once we're assured of approval from another, we feel comfortable enough to drop the facade.

Sometimes, perhaps, we even punish the new friend a little for the strain of our good behavior. Wouldn't the best behavior be a comfortable respect?

My friends deserve my courtesy as well as my love. Today I will welcome them gratefully to my life.

The greatest danger, that of losing one's own self, may pass off quietly as if it were nothing; every other loss, that of an arm, a leg, five dollars, etc., is sure to be noticed.
—Søren Kierkegaard

Loss of self can threaten us at every juncture in a relationship. Self-love and self-acceptance serve as valuable antidotes. None of us is without the need for love and attention from others, and the temptation to buy that love by denying our own needs or goals is great. Dependence on someone else's acknowledgment of our value can be addicting.

We can build self-love. We can create habits that will foster a strong self-image—one that doesn't rely on another's attention to ensure its survival. Self-talk is one tool that promises a changed attitude. When self-talk is positive, we will discover a more secure person. Another tool is imaging. When we image ourselves whole, happy, and at peace in our relationships, we prepare ourselves for the eventuality of that state of mind.

Today offers time to practice becoming a stronger self. My words and my thoughts are my protectors.

June 19

I think I must let go. Must fear not, must be quiet so that my children can hear the Sound of Creation and dance the dance that is in them.

—Russell Hoban

Often we hold fast to our fear, and it prevents us from growing. Life's ordinary rhythm carries us through good times and bad, but sometimes we fear the bad times so much that we try to hold back life's forward motion. This also means that we won't leave ourselves open to the good. The only constant truth is that everything changes. If we can believe in that, it will help us to relax our grip.

Our fear is even stronger when we think we are responsible for others—our children, for example. We want to spare them pain, and so we forget to listen to the Sound of Creation. No one learns from someone else's mistake. If we respect others, we must recognize that they have a right to their own dance. Their own spirits will guide them.

It is often hard to watch another stumble or fall. "I could have spared that tumble!" I may think. But I am wrong. I will trust in others' respect for life.

Change of scene has no effect upon unconscious conflicts.
　　　　　　—Edmund Bergler, M.D.

There's no running away from the internal strife. Whatever haunts us must finally be confronted and resolved if we're ever to grow and thus contribute to our world its due. When we keep secrets locked away, the secrets begin to keep us locked away as well.

It is folly, and yet entirely human, to think a new location, a new job, a new lover will cure whatever troubles us. The truth is, however, that whatever trips us up is at the same time trying to edge us forward to new awareness, and thus the next level of growth. Our troubles are tools for a strengthened foundation. Without them, we'd soon crumble.

When we consider the conflicts we encounter as opportunities for further development, they excite us rather than provoke anxiety. Changing our perspective can make the same scene appear quite new.

As I look out upon "the scene" today, I can control my response to it. I can relish it and grow.

May the new week come to us
For health, life and all good;
May it bring us sustenance, good tidings,
Deliverance and consolations.
     —Women's Sabbath Prayer

Our life constantly renews itself; we celebrate the new year, the new week, the new seasons. New babies, new jobs, new homes give us occasion for rejoicing; the reunions with old friends and family, the strengthening of old bonds, remind us of other cycles of renewal.

For some women, their menstrual cycle provides a silent rhythm of renewal. Some people chart their biorhythm, hoping to tap the ancient springs of life-cycle energy that power the universe. Recovery from an illness, completion of a long project, harvesting a garden, even making a new garment, remind us of our place in the long breathing rhythms of life.

When we are at the end of a cycle, we sometimes forget that renewal always comes. When our energy ebbs, when all the trees are bare, when any effort seems fruitless, we may believe that we have fallen out of the pattern. "I'll never smile again," we think; "the sun's gone out—nothing is worthwhile." Depression for some of us is part of the cycle, and like hibernations or the shedding of foliage, it permits us to gather our strength for the next creative leap.

When things look bleak, I will remember that change and renewal are a law of life.

. . . all humans are frightened of their own solitude. Yet only in solitude can we learn to know ourselves, learn to handle our own eternity of aloneness.

—Han Suyin

Being quiet with ourselves lets the inner person surface. Acknowledging the inner voice invites the comfort it can offer. Acknowledging also gifts us with certain guidance needed by our uncertain steps. Our quiet times away from others nurture the soul struggling to safeguard our journey.

In solitude we find serenity securely nestled in the recesses of our mind. We begin to understand that all is well. We begin to see that our way is being lighted. Only in our quiet times can we fully hear the voice assuring us to move forward, not alone, but in concert with it.

In solitude we find our sanity when the world around us seems insane.

I will go within today in search of rest and peace. I will discover myself.

*All weddings are similar, but every marriage is different.
Death comes to everyone, but one mourns alone.*
—John Berger

What wonderful creatures we human beings are—so alike, and yet so different! We can work together; we have built the Pyramids, the Great Wall, the great cathedrals of Europe, the temples of Peru. We can play music, make quilts, run hospitals, program computers. Yet we can also work alone. Each one of us has the power to think, to plan, to carry out projects that are distinctly ours.

We are both interdependent and independent—and both of these characteristics can give us both joy and pain. Sometimes we feel burdened and oppressed by other people. They *need* us, they weigh on us. We think that if only they would leave us alone, we could realize our true potential.

At other times we feel desperately, achingly alone. Unsupported, abandoned, at such times we may think that if only we had someone on our side, if only someone cared, we would succeed. True freedom, however, like true security, lies within us. We cannot get them from others; we must find them in ourselves.

I will accept either good company or solitude as the condition necessary for self-fulfillment in today's endeavors.

The grand essentials to happiness in this life are something to do, something to love and something to hope for.
—Joseph Addison

Focusing our attention outside of ourselves on hobbies, on goals, on friends, steadily bathes us with inspiration and enthusiasm for moving forward. And this movement, in turn, rekindles our commitment to all our attention-drawing activities.

It is true that happiness lies within us, but our discovery of this is only made possible by our willing involvement in the lives and experiences surrounding us. Those who lead narrow, self-seeking, self-serving lives fail to discover happiness. It lies beyond their reach because they've failed to reach beyond themselves.

Each day is as full and as ripe with adventure and meaning as we choose to make it. Where we look, what we see, do, and plan for, are in our control.

I am personally responsible for the happiness I discover. I'll help my search today by getting truly interested in what others are doing.

June 25

The woman I am
is not what you see
I'm not just bones
and crockery

—Dorothy Livesay

As our bodies age, our spirit remains young.
When we look at old people, too often we see
only the "bones and crockery," the disturbing
image of brittle frailty that lies ahead for us
all. Seldom do we take the time to evoke the
ageless spirit of an old person.

Yet those of us who are privileged to have
close relationships with old men and women
see beyond the mask of age. What we often
find there is a distillation of experience, sometimes wisdom, always keen memory, and almost always a fresh and ruthless impatience
with hypocrisy and lies.

Old people are wonderfully shameless; they
have no time for false pride or prudery. In the
process of living so many years, whatever pre-
tensions they might have had seem to have
dried up and blown away, like corn husks or
last summer's leaves. This quality is as bracing
as sea air.

The very old share it with the very young,
who are too new in the world to be polite.
The lessons that old people can teach us aren't
written anywhere.

Today I will become both old and young by see-
ing beneath the surface.

The universe is transformation; our life is what our thoughts make it.
                              —Marcus Aurelius Antoninus

It's awesome, the power we each wield in the life that unfolds before us. The inclination of our thoughts invites that which we encounter, which is that which we expect to find. What we can become or experience is limited only by our imagination. Our dreams shine like beacons in the dimness of our minds.

Just as our thoughts can nurture positive experiences and outcomes, negative episodes might be drawn to us, too. We can be sure, though, that we use this individual power to create the flavor of each day as it's met.

Our attitude is the by-product of our thoughts. It is in our attitude that we discover strength or weakness, hope or anxiety, determination or frustration. Alone, we determine whether our attitude will be loving or jaundiced.

The breadth of personal power is awesome. Today will be what I choose to make it. No more and no less.

June 27

Science probes; it does not prove.
—Gregory Bateson

We crave security. Even the most restless and adventurous among us has a need for bedrock certainty about something. Religion fills this need for some; politics or ideas satisfy others. When this need is answered, we can achieve a measure of serenity.

Where does this need come from? Nothing in nature is fixed or constant. We know that our bodies, our surroundings, the air we breathe, are made up of chemical compounds that are always changing, renewing, building up, and breaking down. Change is the only constant. And yet, if our inner reality mirrors this change, we may feel chaotic and unquiet.

All great philosophies and religions share the image of a still point, a final proof. The purpose of meditation is to quiet the mind, to find this still point. It is a human need to imagine something beyond changing reality that is the real certainty, the real assurance.

In a world of shifting, slipping reality, where it sometimes seems that our identity is just part of a data base that one computer error could erase, where city streets and national boundaries change their shape every year, we need all the inner stillness and serenity we can find. Belief in constant values can anchor us. Truth is truth, love is love, and we are what we are. These things are always true for us.

I will cultivate my inner serenity; I will attempt to find my constant truth.

*Anyone who limits her vision to memories of yesterday
is already dead.*

—Lily Langtry

The breadth and attitude of our vision for
today's potential or tomorrow's dream will
profoundly influence what we see at this moment. We have the personal power to chart
our course, to set our goals and to take the
necessary steps for their attainment. We also
have the option to walk backwards, stuck in
yesterday's lost hopes.

Imaging the person we strive to be, coupled
with clear details of the path we feel pulled to
travel, is powerful preparation for the actual
trip to our destination. Conversely, our progress to "anywhere or nowhere" is a direct reflection of our shortsightedness.

The strength of our power to create that
which can be is awesome, thrilling, and de-
manding.

*I look to this day with hope and determination
to say, "Yes, I can leap forward."*

God did not make us to be eaten up by anxiety, but to walk erect, free, unafraid in a world where there is work to do, truth to seek, love to give and win.
— Joseph Fort Newton

Today stands before us with promise. It invites us to fully participate in experiences. That we are alive, that we stand present facing this day, guarantees that we are qualified to handle every challenge that snags our attention. And we need have no fear. The world and all that's in it is spirit-full. We are safe and secure if we'd but believe it.

When we look toward the day with confidence, we tap the inner strength that is ever-present. The more frequently we turn to this strength, the less often we are haunted by pangs of anxiety. Our trust in that strength heightens our faith and our understanding that all is well—always and forever all is well.

Giving up fear offers a freedom that will exhilarate us. Faith, trust, confidence will ready us for any challenge, all experiences.

Nothing needs to make me fearful today. I am here. Therefore, God is here too.

My life, I will not let you go except you bless me, but then I will let you go.

—Isak Dinesen

There is something noble in the spirits of those who battle death, who cling to life. We are all moved by their struggle, yet perhaps it is nobler still to let life go when the time comes.

This makes sense only if we think we can look back on a life lived to the fullest. We wouldn't want to die without knowing we had stretched our limits, inhabited them as largely as we could. Not in a worldly sense, perhaps; spiritual breadth can be as exciting as travel, sport, romance, or achievement. It's the limits of our brain and heart we want to test; for that, we could live in one room.

Not everyone is blessed with robust physical health, but we all have the capacity for spiritual health and adventure. Self-examination and meditation are the tools for self-knowledge and serenity. Unknown adventure awaits us when we seek to know ourselves.

My spiritual journey is the real one in my life. On that road, the true blessings are encountered.

July

July 1

A Feather . . . might accomplish it . . . or a Trifle done in the right Spirit . . .

—Djuna Barnes

Sometimes it seems as though a decision truly hangs in the balance, with such equal values on both sides that the weight of a feather might tip it either way. "I was that close to saying no—or yes—" we say, holding thumb and forefinger a few microns apart.

But that's probably not an accurate version of how we came to make our decision. *That close* may not be close at all; we knew all along what was appropriate. If we let ourselves be still and listen to our private inner voice, we usually know what's right for us to do.

If we find ourselves faced with a lot of decisions that seem only a feather's weight apart, maybe we're not acting according to our ideas of what's right. It might be time to reappraise our values. If we're believing one way and acting another, it might be time to change either our behavior or our belief.

Any obstacles to knowing the right course of action are within me, and so is the right course.

When once estrangement has arisen between those who truly love each other, everything seems to widen the breach.
—Mary Elizabeth Braddon

Intimacy is a bonding agent that softens our exteriors while it hushes the inner rumblings and creates a need for itself. None of us is spared that need. Having at least one other with whom we are intimate heals us, keeps us honest, and strengthens us for whatever lies ahead.

When intimacy is absent from our lives, it's terribly easy to lose ourselves—to lose clarity about our identity, to lose confidence and self-assurance. And these losses contribute both to a strong need for intimacy once again, and to a heightened sense of the risk involved in being open and intimate.

Any time we break the intimate bond, we impede our progress as growing, healthy persons. Mental and emotional health is directly proportionate to how close we allow another person to be to us.

My emotional health today is in my control. I'll let someone in.

July 3

That has not half the power to do me harm, as I have to be hurt.

—William Shakespeare

Each day is steaming with activities around which we choose attitudes and reactions. Any one circumstance might anger us today, even though yesterday it triggered laughter. No event, within itself, has the power to determine our feelings or our reactions. How fortunate that this is so. However, we often pretend exactly the reverse. "He makes me mad!" "You've really hurt my feelings." With ease we refuse to take responsibility for whatever mood we're in.

A sure sign of mental and emotional health is acknowledgment of our personal power—power over our feelings, our attitudes, our behavior in every instance. When we celebrate this power, we are energized; we anticipate, confidently, the situations moving toward us, secure in the knowledge that we can make them beneficial to our growth if we so choose.

How much easier it is to face each new day knowing that it has no power over us.

I go forth today ready to take control of my attitude and my behavior. My day will be just as good as I make it.

I also had nightmares. Somehow all the feelings I didn't feel when each thing had actually happened to me I did feel when I slept.

—Andrea Dworkin

Dreams are messages that we send ourselves about things in our lives that bind deep feelings. Often we find ourselves dreaming scenes from our daily life, ordinary situations that may make us anxious. Sometimes our dreams are images like newspapers, account books, or video screens to show us our fears.

When the events in our lives are dangerous and destructive, we may numb ourselves so that we won't feel the fear or pain they provoke. But our dreams know; our nightmares are an outlet for feelings that we've chosen not to feel.

Our dreams will guide us, if we honor them. We don't have to interpret every last detail of a dream to be able to understand it. The symbols in our dreams are coded, and only we can break the code. When a dream brings us strong feelings, we can usually—if we're honest with ourselves—determine what it's about. Then it's up to us what we do about our lives.

My dreams tell my personal story, and all the feelings in them are mine.

July 5

There is after all no obligation to answer every passing fool according to his folly.

—Elias Canetti

Often we behave as though we were in other people's power—as though we were bound to act in certain ways because others expected it from us without their even asking, or our ever checking.

Perhaps we have a deep need to please the authority figures in our lives because we fear we're not worth much. Let's say, further, that our boss stays late in the office every night. We may feel compelled to stay as long as, or longer than, the boss, out of some wish to prove our loyalty and productivity.

Most of us realize that a challenge doesn't mean we have to fight; an invitation doesn't mean we have to accept. But sometimes, especially when it hits a sensitive or insecure area, we find ourselves blindly reacting to someone else's unreasonable actions. We feel sucked in, manipulated, powerless.

We can depend on our own power when we trust in our innate value as humans, and we will make decisions that leave us comfortable with ourselves.

I will remember to guard myself against irrational compliance.

Of course, fortune has its part in human affairs, but conduct is really much more important.
—Jeanne Detourbey

Our behavior in small, mean situations is ultimately as grave in its impact on the whole of human relationships as a major action taken in response to a large-scale crisis. No action or expressed attitude is void of effect. Though it may go unobserved at the time, it will be felt and it will influence another's response at another time.

Our influence on others, on immediate situations, on the future, is profound. When we accept responsibility for all of our actions, as well as our attitudes, our choices will reflect a widened perspective. The power inherent in even the barely perceptible thought is awesome.

My conduct toward others, my unspoken thoughts and unexpressed attitudes will have their effect. My impact today can be positive.

What loneliness is more lonely than distrust?
—George Eliot

Becoming fully trustworthy individuals, living up to our own ideals, makes easier the decision to trust others. And when there is trust, intimacy is possible. With intimacy comes self-love, then other-love, and finally joy.

Isolation from others is a choice, one that breeds new levels of insecurity. Familiarity with isolation hinders our movement toward others, a movement that offers the risk of self-disclosure. And it's this risk that nurtures the friendships that comfort us.

Self-acceptance and self-disclosure are intertwined. Our rough edges are softened and easier to love after we've owned them, held them up for inspection, and patted them before tucking them away.

Today offers new hope to the hopeful. Being rid of the burden of distrust will lighten my day.

Love is when each person is more concerned for the other than for one's self.

—David Frost

Loving ourselves is a healthy and necessary attitude if we are to garner the strength and confidence to move into our world of experiences each day. Self-love, when it is honest and nurturing, fosters compassion toward the others who share our experiences. Preoccupation with self is not self-love.

How distorted our perceptions of life are when, with incessant rigidity, we force our personal selves to the center of every experience. When we focus only on how a situation relates to our own lives, too often we lose sight of the lesson we might have learned. To look instead with compassion upon the needs and frustrations of those sharing our experiences will usher in solutions and will invite an exchange of gratitude which makes all expressions of love easier.

When we look outward with love and acceptance toward our fellow travelers, we inwardly feel greater love, too.

Any expression of real love today—toward anyone—will multiply my possibilities for loving.

July 9

It was only after the advent of the white man that we met people who did not understand about the uniqueness of human beings.

—Good Day

Human beings have been known to act toward other people as though they were things, objects, instead of subjects like ourselves. Men sometimes act this way toward women; parents toward children; the young toward the old. This behavior has been most obvious and brutal toward the original inhabitants of some territory that others wish to colonize.

As the world runs out of secrets, and no place is left open to colonial assaults, we must guard against this tendency among ourselves. We can see it in military organizations and in industrial production, in bureaucracy and in mass movements. It's called disrespect for the individual, and it's always dangerous.

Each human being is precious and unique. It injures our spirit to forget that, even for a moment. And when we remember it, we're better able to act in concert with our self-respecting fellows.

In respecting ourselves fully, we show others how to treat us, and as we treat them respectfully we acknowledge and enhance their humanity. The quality of human interaction can be so wonderful; why should we deface it by forgetting others' uniqueness?

I'll look for the same respect from others, today, that I show them.

By education most have been misled
So they believe, because they so were bred.
The priest continues what the nurse began,
And thus the child imposes on the man.
                                    —John Dryden

In the early years it often seems to the growing human child that most of civilization consists of saying "No!" Parents and teachers sometimes act as if that were so. Everyone who has ever raised, taught, or cared for small children knows what a totally involving commitment it is, and knows, too, that it is impossible to do everything right. Parents struggle with their children over trivia; teachers may punish small infractions and ignore large ones. Humans raise humans; if it were possible to do it perfectly, surely we would all be angels by now.

Often we are fully grown before we're able to let go of some of the rigid rules we learned. Often it may seem that our task as adults is to *un*learn what we learned as infants. The "housebreaking" that has made us considerate to one another and peaceable in adjusting our differences may also have squelched some of our capacity for feeling.

We can recover our feeling selves, without violating the rules of society, if we can remember not to be afraid. Feelings are only frightening when we repress them; when we let them out and let them sweep through, then they are gone.

My feelings may be strong, but they are not evil. How could they be? I am a child of the universe.

Persons who habitually drink water become as fine
gourmets on the subject as wine drinkers on wine.
                              —Alexander Dumas

How fortunate are those among us who have the ability to turn things around—to transform liabilities into assets. Life deals them lemons: they make lemonade, lemon pie, candied lemon peel. They seem to be able to assess the needs of the moment accurately and turn them to advantage.

We are all different. Success in life probably has more to do with expressing our uniqueness fully than with suppressing it and trying to resemble everybody else. Who is "everybody else," anyway?

We can't respond authentically to the moment if we're concealing the truth. The truth for us involves our own unique package of qualities, our own experience and energy, our own way of looking at things. Freedom, for us, depends on the choices only we can make. The proper appreciation of water is a pleasure that demands discipline. We're totally unable to experience this pleasure if we are wishing for wine.

Human beings share many characteristics.
One of the most important is difference. Today
I will cherish these differences as one of the
bonds that joins me to others.

. . . he yearned to package for each of the children, the grandchildren, for everyone, that joyous certainty, that sense of mattering, of moving and being moved, of being one and indivisible with the great of the past, with all that freed, ennobled.

—Tillie Olsen

In childhood we glimpse the dear connectedness of life. The delicious sense that life is a grand adventure mustn't be put away with our roller skates or high school diplomas; it remains as true for us today as it was when we first sniffed freedom and greatness in the air.

Life holds so much! Every morning we can open a package of "that joyous certainty." Each day, as we trace our paths, we're connected with all that has gone before, and all that is presently in the world, and we are preparing the future. Yes, we matter; we matter enormously, each one of us as much as any other; our unique and precious consciousness matters above all things.

The part we play touches all of life. Sometimes we choose to join our personal strength with others'; sometimes we act alone. But we are part of the whole, linked by our lives and our choices to all the others on earth, as they are linked to us.

Today I'll be true to my heritage of freedom and nobility.

July 13

It seems that there is a direct connection between creative thought and involvement in life and the production of epinephrine by the adrenal gland. When the challenge stops, the supply is turned off; the will to live atrophies.
                                        —Norman Cousins

Living on the fringes of activity is a choice we can make. Always holding back, rather than becoming fully intimate with another in conversation is a choice we can make. Partial attention rather than wholehearted involvement with the task at hand, whether it be reading a report, chopping wood, or preparing a meal, is also such a choice. Each moment we choose half-involvement we are also choosing partial death. The soul is nourished only by the rapture of fully experiencing the myriad vibrations surrounding us.

Attuning ourselves to "all that is" elevates the mind, heightens gladness, nurtures the creative act. Each task we undertake today will benefit ourselves and others only to the degree of attention we give it.

The joys today offers are tucked inside the experiences that invite my attention. Living on life's fringes won't bring joy.

*If we try too hard to force others to live in our world, be-
cause we think it is the real world, we are doomed to disappointment.*

—William Glasser, M.D.

The desire to control other people, all situations and each outcome to benefit ourselves is
a human compulsion, and one destined to foster frustration. Our need to control others is
addicting, but our condition is not hopeless.

"Letting go" is a learned behavior. Like any
habit, practice will make it a natural response.
Freedom to fully respond to any experience
can only be attained when we have sacrificed
the outcome to whatever the bigger picture
dictates.

To be enthusiastically, creatively alive means
responding to the pulse of the moment, which
means following the unself-conscious inner
urging rather than the self-protecting and
consciously manipulative ego. Our burdens
are lightened each time we act free from the
weight of the ego.

*Letting go of others will lift my own spirit high
today.*

Our ordinary mind always tries to persuade us that we are nothing but acorns and that our greatest happiness will be to become bigger, fatter, shinier acorns; but that is of interest only to pigs. Our faith gives us knowledge of something much better: that we can become oak trees.
—E. F. Schumacher

Most of us struggle at times with a sense of worthlessness. Sometimes this sense of being good for nothing leads us to self-destructive behavior; sometimes it is accompanied by self-pity. At such times, other people's lives appear infinitely attractive, and we may fancy that there are easy solutions to our problems. "If only I had two nice children, an adoring spouse, and a house in the suburbs!" we may think, or "Oh, to be single and on my own in the big city!"

The truth is, and we know it when we're not in a funk, that our solutions, like our problems, lie within us. We all tend to blame other people and circumstances for our own shortcomings. That's human. But we let go of blaming if we want to grow.

We have the power to transform every situation. If we feel trapped by a job that seems dull or a relationship that seems lifeless, we can redefine our sense of the trap. What do we want? What prevents our going after it? What opportunities have we overlooked? If we're frightened by a prospect that seems dangerous, we can turn it into a challenge, and at the same time plan realistically how to protect ourselves.

I will remember that every seeming problem is an opportunity for growth.

Sharing a burdened heart with another who has the wisdom, strength, and knowledge to carry it, frees us from its weight long enough to focus on solutions.
—Liane Cordes

Our obsession with a problem, any incessant problem, keeps it a problem. Our focus on it destroys the balanced perspective that is necessary for a solution to become apparent. Sharing a problem's details with an interested friend clarifies the muddle. It also doubles the chances that a solution will emerge.

Holding onto problems, like keeping secrets, keeps us stuck. Our emotional health is proportionate to the freedom with which we willingly share ourselves with the people close to us. Sharing our joys doubles them. Sharing our burdens diminishes them. But more than that, it promises the discovery of their solutions.

Today I will share a problem, perhaps my own or someone else's. A solution will be apparent, nevertheless.

You had better live your best and act your best and think your best today; for today is the sure preparation for tomorrow and all the other tomorrows that follow.
—Harriet Martineau

What's done is done. What's been said is said. We can't undo the mistakes of yesterday. And occasionally they create the barriers blocking us today. However, we can make sure that our behavior today doesn't contribute to unnecessary problems for tomorrow.

A negative attitude toward other people and toward life's circumstances becomes habitual. Fortunately, a positive attitude does as well. The choice rests with each of us to respond in ways fitting to the preferred attitude.

How much easier all situations are when we are respectful, hopeful, and interested. Likewise, the trivial matter can become a major catastrophe when we struggle unnecessarily and with carping egos. We make the world we find, at home, at work, and at play.

Today is mine to make. Let me choose my attitude with care.

Man is a pliant animal—a being who gets accustomed to anything.

—Fyodor Dostoyevsky

The ease with which we adapt to our surroundings is, to some degree, a very positive trait. It means we are generally flexible. However, our pliancy may allow us to adjust to situations that harm us. We learn with too much ease to accept painful situations—maybe believing that time will ease us away from it, or that a bit of magic will transform the people and the situation, thus eliminating the pain.

Knowing when to adapt to circumstances and when to make a personal choice to move away takes mature assessment. It also takes attunement to our inner self—the "knower" of all right action. Development of this relationship with our inner selves takes practice, courage, patience, and the willingness to detach our minds from external stimuli for a time. Responsible choices are never accidental reactions, and they will sometimes usher in a radical action, at other times easy acceptance.

Today will offer opportunities to "go along with" a situation. I will be thoughtful rather than always pliant.

. . . [I]f you listen carefully, you get to hear everything you didn't want to hear in the first place.
                                        —Sholom Aleichem

What are those things that we don't want to hear? Mainly, we don't want to hear disagreement from people who are important to us. We don't want to hear that our children are making choices we wouldn't make; we don't want to hear that our partner believes we are anything but perfect; we don't want to hear that our friend, our parent, our teacher, our boss, sees anything in us to criticize.

Poor us! We know we aren't perfect, but we can't tolerate hearing it from someone else. Why should that be? We know other people aren't perfect, either. Where did we get the idea that we're supposed to be error-free?

To accept our own imperfection is to make a giant step toward peace of mind. To accept that the world is full of people who disagree with us—some of whom even love us very much—is to begin to achieve maturity. Perhaps we think, or used to think, that we would be happy when we rubbed out our last traces of imperfection. That is not happiness, that is to become marble—hard, cold, and breakable.

True spiritual progress begins with my acceptance of my imperfections.

Our soul makes constant noise, but it has a silent place we never hear.

—Simone Weil

In an unjust, difficult world, our soul is often in pain and weeping. Sometimes it makes a joyful noise. But the silent place, the still center, is one we may neglect. Like white light, this silence of the soul contains everything, yet it transfers the warring jumble of noise and color into a peaceful blankness.

Call it acceptance or surrender. The stillness of the spirit is the stillness of communion with truth beyond change. It's silent because it doesn't belong to the world of the senses. We have spiritual knowledge that's ancient, if we let ourselves listen to it, and it will nourish us, if we permit.

For some of us, it's a great effort just to learn to listen to the noise of our souls. We've spent years blotting out pain or joy with alcohol, other drugs, or rationalizations. We feel we've made enormous progress when we learn to hear our own soul's noise. But be assured, the soul's great silence can be achieved. It's our choice.

My spirit can grow infinitely. I trust where it will take me.

Grief can take care of itself, but to get the full value of joy you must have somebody to divide it with.
　　　　　　　　　　　—Mark Twain

We share this planet that supports us. We share it with other living creatures, each one offering a necessary ingredient that nurtures and sustains the continuation of the whole. Every experience that involves one of us, involves others who also need what the experience may teach. We are not alone, ever. We are traveling a path in concert with others whose needs are similar to our own.

We can expect to discover joyous occasions and will undoubtedly be visited by grief in our travels. The latter will be eased by the knowledge that others, too, have known grief. Joy, on the other hand, is doubled in intensity when we acknowledge the occasion giving birth to it and then celebrate it with others. No day passes without giving us many occasions to shout for joy. Too often, feeling alone and lonely, we close our eyes to the wonders that could excite us. The most fruitful lesson we can learn is that we have fellow travelers among whom joy abounds and multiplies when shared.

Today I'll look for the joy in my life.

*As contagion
of sickness makes sickness,
contagion of trust can make trust.*
                                        —Marianne Moore

Attitudes give birth to themselves. Fresh ideas
foster fresh responses to old and new situations. Each of us is favored with responses
from others that generally match those we've
shared, too. We should never be surprised by
how others treat us. We have been their teachers in every instance. Giving love invites it.
Expression of honesty encourages that, too.
We must only expect that hatefulness and dis-
honesty will greet us if we've offered nothing
more to others.

   We should always be aware of the power
of our attitudes and behavior toward others.
They will bring favor or disfavor upon us. We
should be mindful, too, that joy is contagious—
as are respectful behavior, a trusting attitude,
and gratitude. We are charged with the responsibility for creating a better world in which
to live. Peace and happiness begin here, now,
with each of us.

*Peace, joy, and good fortune will accompany
me on my trip today if I do my individual part
to spread it.*

Not the fruit of experience, but experience itself, is the end.
—Walter Pater

The end can never justify the means; the means is life, as we live it, in the present moment. When we read of aged paupers who die on a bare mattress stuffed with cash, we recognize their delusion; but at times we can lose that clarity and find ourselves justifying practices that we know are undesirable in the service of a desired end.

Means that involve injustice or deprivation are never justifiable. We cannot ignore experience. We may have our sights set on a law degree or a sports car, but the experience of law school and of budgeting for the car are what we live. The quality of our life isn't measured by our degrees or possessions but by our behavior. If we have love and fulfilling work, nothing else matters.

Let's concentrate on today; it's all we have. Within this day, we have many choices and a rich texture of experience. We can't control the outcome; the moment is within our grasp. We must seize it, savor it, learn from it; it is life itself.

If I were meant to live in the future, my eyes would have telescopic lenses.

Two great human institutions were apparently inaugurated together, proprietary marriage and the division of society into masters and servants.
—Emily James Putnam

Just as every generation must invent sex for itself, so every committed relationship must invent equality. The concept is an old one; histories and civics books are full of it; but most of us have precious little experience of it in our lives.

Unfortunately, most of life is some variation of a dominant-subordinate relation. However loving our parents and teachers, they definitely have the upper hand. We play games to win; we're ranked in school and at work. We learn to jockey for position, to manipulate, to get what we want from those we perceive as above us and below us on the scales.

For many of us, intimate relationships present a new challenge: how to get along as an equal. With no assumption of superiority or inferiority, sometimes we're at a loss. How does one act with an equal? Who gets to decide? What are the rules?

Emotional openness, honesty, and willingness to take risks can bring most of us to the point where we can share equally—or, at least, discuss the issues with a partner. It's hard to let go of our old place on the ladder—to decide to be neither a master nor a servant.

Rare is the experience of equality. I will let myself be open to it.

July 25

The question is laid out
For each of us to ask:
Whether to hold on
Or to drop the mask.

—Martha Boesing

Do you ever feel you are wearing a mask? It's a strange, uncomfortable feeling. We mistrust our own face; we don't even know what it looks like, because we put on the mask so young. But sooner or later we must drop it and face our reflection.

Perhaps the mask is silent, and behind it we feel like screaming. Perhaps the mask is festive, and our own eyes weep.

The mask chafes and confines us, but it gives protection, too. We're naked without it; we have nowhere to hide. To summon the courage to drop the mask, we must believe in ourselves enough to trust our naked vulnerability.

We may take courage in knowing that everyone is vulnerable and afraid. By wearing our own faces proudly, we show that it's possible. Soon, masks will be dropping all around.

Today I will risk showing myself as I really am.

The principle of life is that life responds by corresponding;
your life becomes the thing you have decided it shall be.
—Raymond Charles Barker

The attitude that we carry with us into a particular setting will greatly influence our perceptions of any event. Our attitude also influences,
positively or negatively, personal interactions,
and not just those involving ourselves. The effect of our message is this: our personal power
is profound. We have explicit control over our
own perceptions. We determine our own attitudes. Every moment of our lives we are deciding what we want to see, to think, to feel.
And reflections will inform us that our expectations are firmly fulfilled.

How exhilarating to become aware of our
freedom to think and to feel as we wish. However, with this freedom comes responsibility.
We're barred from blaming others for our
troubles. Each of us is charged with the responsibility for deciding our own fate. How
we prepare ourselves for this experience or
this day is individually chosen. Every minute
we are in control of our perceptions, our attitudes, our responses.

Today is mine to mold. My attitude, my
thoughts and responses will decide my fate
today.

Whoever is interested in life is particularly interested in death.

—Thomas Mann

In this biological world we can see clearly that death is a stage in the life cycle. In our human case, we cling to the precious consciousness that seems to set us apart from the rest of the natural world, and we see death with different eyes—as an ending, often cruel, and sometimes unendurable.

We do ourselves no service to make an enemy of death; it is a presence within our life, and by denying it, we deny a part of ourselves. Our deepest knowledge includes a knowledge of death. To experience loss and to grieve it are the great common human experiences, and to deny them is to make ourselves less human.

We live in a beautifully balanced system in which death is a part of everything that lives. The pain of our personal loss is ours; within the greater whole, nothing is lost. Perhaps it is too much to say that we will ever understand death; the fruit of time and pain and healing is that we will come to accept it.

Let me open myself to the knowledge of wisdom, to which death belongs in equal measure with life.

If you find your inner conversation running along negative lines, you have the power to change the subject, to think along different lines.

—Martha Smock

Most of us carry on a continual inner dialogue. At times we're sizing up our co-workers or perhaps strangers entering the room. At other times we're being critical of our appearance, or a piece of work we've just completed, or of our capabilities to handle a new challenge that's in our path. If we were to log the minutes of self-talk and categorize them, many of us might discover that few moments of the inner dialogue are supportive or filled with praise. In fact, we often verbally abuse ourselves and others—a behavior we can ill afford.

Determination to change our inner thoughts is our first step, if we want to find greater peace and happiness in this life. We are under no one's power but our own, and we have chosen negative thinking for whatever payoff it offered. Time will prove to us that the payoffs from positive thinking are far greater. We tend to become the person our thoughts prepare us to be.

I will celebrate my personal power and use it to my advantage. Today!

July 29

. . . we have
grown into one as we slept and
now I can't jump
because I can't let go your hand.

—Marina Tsvetayeva

Long, intimate relationships often confuse us. We may lose the sense of where our individual boundaries are. We confuse our desires and our pain with another person's—our spouse or lover, our parent, siblings, or child. When that relationship changes, when the other person dies or leaves or forms another intimate bond, we may feel wounded and desperate, unsure of who we are.

The blurring of boundaries is never healthy for us—although we may not feel the damage at first. Sound relationships are carefully made; we enter into them without giving away our own authentic responses to life. When relationships change, of course we may feel pain; but we need not feel the awful confusion that comes from having given pieces of ourselves away.

I'll adjust my focus so there are no blurred areas in my relationships. For me to love well, I need to know where I stand.

Everything has its own perfection, be it higher or lower in the scale of things; and the perfection of one is not the perfection of another.

—John Henry Newman

There is no "perfection" in the world, yet in another sense, everything is perfect. Everything has its part to play in the world's great unfolding.

Everything in our lives serves its purpose for us. Everyone we meet today will bear some message that we need to hear—just as we'll bring messages to others. We're all partners in this dance. Each move we make affects the whole pattern, and we respond to the changes made by one another.

Sometimes the message is a need for change. That message is perfect, too. At each moment we are where we need to be, and the path before us can be clear. If we don't see it, it's because we've chosen not to.

When we grasp the reality of choice and change, when we learn to live in the moment, we come to understand perfection not as a frozen, changeless state, but as a part of our perpetual becoming. May the next perfect moment carry us to ever more satisfying choices.

Today I'll strive to clear my path and to appreciate the perfection of each moment that I choose.

We are whole beings. We know this somewhere in a part of ourselves that feels like memory.
                                        —Susan Griffin

When we study biology, we learn that in every cell of our bodies we carry our whole genetic program, the complex set of chemical instructions for building us: our skeleton, skin, hair, eyes, muscles, brain, genitals, guts. Every human being is born with a set of capacities and responses that are as much a part of him or her as the capacity to grow fingernails or to heal cuts.

Yet deep in our language and culture is a habit of speaking about ourselves as though our intelligence, our feelings, and our will could be separated from the rest of us. We talk about "a body/mind split," as though our bodies or our minds did not fully belong to us. And all cultures have the myth of a golden age when humans were fully integrated.

Much "civilized" behavior is bad for us— we eat and breathe stuff that no self-respecting animal would tolerate. Our lives can make us ill: immobility, anxiety, and stress show up as ulcers, hypertension, skin rashes, heart disease, obesity. We need to learn to respect ourselves as animals, and not to deny that we have bodies. Our lives, like ourselves, are all of one piece, whether or not we understand.

My real golden age is now, because it is the only time I have.

August

August 1

Keep your face to the sunshine and you cannot see the shadow.

        —Helen Keller

We can make of our experiences what we choose. We can focus on the traffic snarls while traveling to work, or we can smile because we have a job to go to and a car to carry us there. We can be angry because the washing machine broke down, or grateful that we've been free, for a while, of the laundromat hassle. Every experience offers us an opportunity to respond, and our response is always a reflection of our emotions.

We choose to be angry, depressed, or afraid. We can just as easily decide to be trusting, happy, or confident. And the exciting realization for us is that we are free to choose whatever pleases us. Even though we've gotten mad for years over traffic jams doesn't mean we can't give up the anger. How liberating it is to claim control of our emotions, our attitudes, our reactions to the full panorama of our experiences.

Today can trip me up or I can run with it, leading all the way.

Old folks—and here I'm talking about myself—need more than anything else to feel they are needed, that they have a purpose in life.

—Ruth Youngdahl Nelson

Believing that we count in the lives of others, that others need us and appreciate our contribution in the workplace, the community, and at home is a universal need. In those times when reassurance from others is lacking, we must simply remember that every one of us is unique, and created to contribute to our surroundings in individually inspired ways. At every moment we are leveling an impact on the physical, mental, and emotional environment of the community that surrounds us.

We are not without purpose. The daily activities which invite our attention are the paths to growth and fulfillment which are fitting for the contributions we are called on to offer. We are obliged to do our part.

My involvement in life has meaning. I may not wholly understand the part I'm playing but I can trust that I'm being invited, today, to participate in matters influencing a bigger picture.

August 3

Any idea seriously entertained tends to bring about the realization of itself.
                                        —Joseph Chilton Pearce

There is magic in believing in our capabilities at the moment, believing in our future potential, believing that we are worthy human beings with a purpose for being alive. Those ideas we hold in our minds, be they positive self-appraisals or negative personal assessments, will influence our behavior and as a consequence will invite others to form like-minded opinions. We tell others what to think of us by our actions and reactions, silences and outbursts.

However, the chance is present every moment to realize new dreams, to progress to new heights, to switch whatever course we are presently traveling on. All it takes is a changed attitude, commitment to a new idea, and the accompanying belief in the idea's potential. Any idea held in our mind can become a reality.

I'll have a chance to practice believing in myself and my potential today. It will open new doors.

Rivers and roads lead people on.
> —Georgia O'Keeffe

Life is flowing and continuous; it is full of crossroads, tributaries, and sudden bends. To live is to travel, and navigable space attracts us. We want to follow the road or the river to find what lies around the next bend, over the next rise. The mere fact that they exist seems to tell us that we should follow them.

No one has ever lived our lives before us. This moment we are in a space and time that have never been traveled. Many past events prepared us for this moment, and we may often feel as though we were following a track that has been laid out for us; but at other times we feel as though we were strapped to the nose of a rocket, plunging through space where no one has ever been.

Then, at times (and we wish they were less rare), we become one with our path, immersed in our lives unquestioningly. This is the condition we prefer; when the river that leads us through life simply flows.

I will endeavor to accept my life; it is taking me where I need to go.

August 5

You cannot shake hands with a clenched fist.
                              —Indira Gandhi

Each person we welcome into our lives blesses us in ways that only the passage of time can validate. To invite someone in, however, takes an honest extension of the self, an open-armed posture which implies that we will risk being open.

How short and bland life seems when we cut ourselves off from the myriad experiences and acquaintances that present themselves to us. When we back away from the persons who have curiously crossed our paths, we back away from the lessons for which earlier experiences and persons have prepared us. Our progress and our success in life is both measured and nurtured by the number of genuine contacts we make with the men and women who are sharing our space in time.

Will I offer myself freely to today's experiences and personalities? The choice is mine.

So get a few laughs and do the best you can. Don't have an ideal to work for. That's like riding towards the mirage of a lake.

—Will Rogers

Human societies seem to go from crisis to crisis, fraught with injustice, oppression, and deception. But comedy is a gift of the human spirit. Sometimes it is the only weapon we have against official absurdity. Doesn't it often seem as though those who most clearly understand the dangers that face us are the ones who can play most wholeheartedly?

Laughter and play don't mean carelessness. Each of us must make our way through these serious times, carefully ordering our priorities and doing what we need to do to safeguard our spiritual growth. One temptation that besets many of us is to take ourselves so seriously that we begin to attach great weight to unimportant gestures. Humor is a wonderful tool for shaping us back down to size.

Sharing play is sometimes the only way we can touch another human being. Let us be grateful for the gift of true humor wherever we encounter it. It gives us strength to continue.

Today's events will remind me who I am. I will accept them with humor.

August 7

There is guidance for each of us, and by lowly listening, we shall hear the right word.
                              —Ralph Waldo Emerson

Perhaps it was only yesterday or the day before that we doubted our value to society, or to our family or friends. We often lose our direction. That's normal and consistent with the human condition. However, the length of time we spend floundering, uncertain of ourselves, is proportionate to the time it takes us to acknowledge the guide within. We need not be lost or full of doubt for long.

Going within ourselves may not be a spontaneous reaction for many of us, but we can learn to respond in this way. And when we're open to the inner urging and willing to follow it, we'll discover the benefits. All that's asked of us is the decision to listen.

I can quiet my thoughts today, long enough to sense the necessary direction to take. I can be certain the guidance is right for me.

Everyone has a talent. What is rare is the courage to follow the talent to the dark place where it leads.
—Erica Jong

Our lives are purposeful and the dreams that mold our actions or tease us down new avenues are not coincidental. Our dreams are messages from the inner self, who urges us to fulfill the purpose for which our talents have been given. We each have talents to be employed in a fashion uniquely our own; however, all too many of us opt for the half-life, never fully giving our attention to the occasion at hand.

We can never know our talents or when to utilize them when we pass through life on the fringe of activities. We cut off our awareness of the inner urging when we don't enter into the present, when we step back from ourselves, when we refrain from offering rapt attention to the "talent scouts" among us. And we'll never experience the joy we deserve until we favor the inhabitants of our world with our talent.

My dreams are my guides but I must follow them.

August 9

. . . there are many sham diamonds in this life which pass for real, and vice versa, many real diamonds which go unvalued.

—W. M. Thackeray

It's high praise to say that someone is "genuine—the real thing." We use the image of jewelry when we talk about character: "Pure gold—14 karat—rings true—a diamond of the first water—a pearl." The qualities of beauty and rarity make gems precious to us, and by using the same language to describe people, we imply that real personal worth is equally beautiful, and equally rare.

Yet it's within everyone's grasp. We all agree on the valuable character traits: honesty, loyalty, openness, courage, humor, and the capacity for love. Everyone has them, and everyone can have them. Imitations won't do.

I needn't worry about whether someone else's qualities are genuine. I know what I admire and I have plenty to do polishing my own.

It is possible to be different and still be all right. There can be two—or more—answers to the same question, and all can be right.

—Anne Wilson Schaef

We're accustomed to thinking there are two sides to a subject: right/wrong, Democrat/Republican, walk/don't walk. This binary mode of thinking may lead us to disregard many possible solutions to our problems. "That's what makes ball games," we say, as though life were a competitive game. Relationships are an area where many of us fail to recognize that a question can have many right answers.

We may find ourselves locked into behavior patterns that guarantee we will be unhappy. We may set ourselves up as victims: "Everything happens to me!" or as bullies: "They all *obey* me, but no one *likes* me."

If we look at our own part, we often can see that if we had behaved differently in a situation, the outcome might have been different. We often act as though we were programmed in a simple binary mode, yet we have the power to choose a new mode at any moment.

Today I will be true to my reality, which offers me an infinite range of choices.

When you are offended at any man's fault, turn to yourself and study your own failings. Then you will forget your anger.

—Epictetus

We take note of others' shortcomings and frequently record them in our minds, and then rely on these memories to feel superior. Seldom do we perceive our own failings as clearly. It takes courage and determination to inventory all our traits, both the pleasant and the unpleasant. It also takes an honest desire to know ourselves before we can fully assess the value of our traits. We can be certain, however, that the shortcomings we've noticed in others, we'll discover in ourselves.

It might well be a worthwhile exercise in personal development to let what bothers us in others guide our own attempt at self-improvement. For instance, if another's cynicism triggers negative feelings in us, we can be fairly certain we, too, respond cynically on occasion. Then we can make the decision to clean our own house. We aren't perfect, but we can strive to like ourselves, and others. Self-improvement and self-love will make it easier to accept someone else.

If I don't like something someone is doing today, I will take an honest look at myself.

. . . words are more powerful than perhaps anyone suspects, and once deeply engraved in a child's mind, they are not easily eradicated.

—May Sarton

Some of our greatest adult sufferings are owed to the many innocent abuses inflicted upon us as children. Harsh words, demeaning punishments, too many silent treatments, taught us who we were. Many of us remain disheartened, even diminished because of these powerful memories. When we accept criticism as accurate and deserved, it molds our characters, and eventually we live up to these assessments.

The good news is that we are in control of our own thoughts and attitudes, and in this respect we are all-powerful. The decision is ours to cast aside another's criticism, replacing it with positive self-talk. However, to successfully undo the harm others' words have caused takes daily dedication to our own positive reinforcement. Those who are confident and assured have internalized a positive dialogue with themselves.

Today is a new beginning, and I can make a fresh start by believing that I am a worthwhile person and my contribution is necessary.

*. . . it is only by labour that thought can be made healthy,
and only by thought that labour can be made happy, and
the two cannot be separated with impunity.*
                                        —John Ruskin

We all require a balance of thought and labor,
intellectual and muscular effort in our lives.
The work that most of us do doesn't exercise
either our brains or our bodies fully. Most of
us aren't scientists or scholars, or farmers or
dancers; we spend our working lives doing
routine tasks and our leisure time on passive
amusements.

It's within our power to enhance the quality
of our health and happiness. If we look around,
the world is full of challenges to our minds
and bodies. We need only open ourselves to
them. Other people will welcome what we can
give—physical effort, mental gymnastics, or
any combination of the two.

Ideas that aren't applied or tested tend to
become anemic; and work that isn't examined
and evaluated tends to become stale. We can't
really separate our minds from our bodies
without injuring them both. Our knowledge
that we are whole, integral beings is precious;
let it illuminate this day.

*My spiritual well-being depends on living
deeply with both my thought and my labor.*

To find the good life you must become yourself.
—Dr. Bill Jackson

The more we run away from ourselves, the greater is our disenchantment with all the opportunities each day offers. When we live far from our own center, we ensure distance from all the persons in our life. Happiness in all things eludes us when we become distant from self and others.

Finding ourselves, closing the gap on the distance created, is a by-product of a personal inventory. We must *know* our wholeness before we can celebrate ourselves. And with celebration comes relief, freedom, and a readiness to tackle the opportunities presented to us.

Self-acceptance fosters self-love—the necessary prerequisite to the discovery of a good life. It's within reach. We must decide to move wholly toward it.

I can be excited about the chance to celebrate myself today. My qualities are special and deserve recognition.

If politics may be broadly defined as "the way we are with each other" then anything that affects how we connect with each other is political.

—Phyllis Jane Rose

There's a word for someone who is democratic with strangers and despotic with intimates, and the word is hypocrite. One of the important lessons of our time is that the personal is political. Our behavior reveals our true beliefs and what we truly are.

"Politics" may sound like too heavy a word for our behavior with our families, lovers, friends, and co-workers. Yet it's accurate. If we oppress or manipulate those who are close to us, bribing and threatening instead of asking honestly and negotiating for what we want, then it doesn't matter what we say, or how we vote. Our weakness and lack of maturity reveal us to be unstable.

Our politics is our lives: how we connect with one another, how we use resources, even how we think about things. How we deal with the smallest details is how we really are, and others are apt to deal with us in kind. If we're abusive or insincere, we're going to encounter abuse and insincerity. Let's bring our behavior into agreement with our beliefs.

Today I'll tune in to my political broadcast and make sure it reflects my platform.

Any path is only a path, and there is no affront, to oneself or to others, in dropping it if that is what your heart tells you.

—Carlos Castaneda

Our inner guide, our conscience, desires to be heard every step of our way today. And the choice to listen is easy if we've developed trust in those messages from our heart. There is no absolute path we need to follow in this life, but some will be more advantageous to our destiny than others. And some paths will weave themselves more smoothly among the paths of other travelers. We are all moving toward the same destination.

How thrilling it is to recognize that there is a message center within that has foreknowledge of our needs today, of the direction most fitting to the growth that's in store presently. We are not lonely, forgotten figures in this universe. We have purpose. And we can fulfill our purpose if we are acting in concert with our heart's message. When we move softly through the day, we can be certain of hearing the words forming within.

I'll take slow, sure steps today and know I'm on the right path.

We only do well the things we like doing.

—Colette

When you were a child, did you feel you had to do everything you were told to do? If you didn't perform all tasks equally well, did you feel that something was wrong with you?

When we were young, many of us were never told that we were doing as well as we could. Or if we were told, we didn't know how to hear it. It has taken some of us years to learn that to do something well often means to do it as well as we can. And somewhere inside us, those children still groan over tasks they can't do easily.

It helps to remember that we are not alone. Something we find difficult to do may have all sorts of repercussions for us and for others. We can always ask for help. Other people are pleased when we ask them to share their skills. When we know how to console the child within, we need never feel inadequate.

I'm working toward the day when I can truthfully say, "I like everything I do because I do everything as well as I can."

. . . the healthy, the strong individual, is the one who asks for help when he needs it whether he's got an abscess on his knee or in his soul.

—Rona Barrett

It is not meant that we should shoulder our problems alone. We are in the company of others by design, and the growth that each of us needs to experience is tied closely to both the sufferings and the celebrations that come to us all.

We each have the capacity to nurture and guide another's wavering steps. But the invitation to help must be extended. Perhaps we need reminding that each of us carries within us the remedy for another's ills. Likewise, someone among us awaits our call for help. We are accompanying one another on this journey because together we can smooth away the rough spots that would cause us to stumble if we were traveling alone.

Many calls for help will be made today, and some of us will be ready to respond. All of us need to remember that one of our greatest gifts is offering comfort to our stumbling friends.

Others need to help me—just as much as I may need their help.

August 19

A truly total history would cancel itself out—its product would be nought.

—Claude Lévi-Strauss

The world has always been as rich and varied as it is at this moment. Wealth and poverty, joy and pain, peace and struggle, have always existed side by side. The history of human life is the history of each person's journey from birth to death.

When we study history, we're always reading someone's interpretation or argument. The total history could never argue a point or prove an interpretation. We each can tell many true stories about ourselves by selecting facts from our personal histories. Yet our total history will cancel these stories and show us to be neither saints nor villains, merely seekers.

There's much we can learn from others' stories. They can illuminate our path; they can persuade us of the wisdom of one choice or another. Yet to be fully human is to escape the neat outlines of such a story. We immerse ourselves in life; we are surrounded by it.

I will try to respect everyone's reality, and to remember that much of the world lies outside my range of vision.

The liar leads an existence of unutterable loneliness.
—Adrienne Rich

All human interactions are built on agreement. Language itself depends on agreement: we agree, broadly, on the meaning of friend, blue, danger, cold. We agree on times of meeting, rules of procedure, and appropriate behaviors for many situations.

To lie is to break some of those agreements. "I returned your call" is a harmless lie, we might think, but if we didn't return the call, then we're lying about our intentions and our actions. It would be so much simpler for us to say, "I meant to return your call." So why don't we?

One important motive for telling such lies is to make ourselves look good. "I returned your call"; "I don't know how the paint got chipped"; "Someone stole my gloves"; all these are small falsehoods in which we claim that our performance was error-free—whatever slippage occurred wasn't our fault.

Human beings aren't error-free. We forget things, mislay our gloves, back into telephone poles. We're human. Pretending we're not isolates us from the rest of humanity. Not only do we break the agreement at the base of language, we set ourselves apart from each other. We pretend we are more perfect than someone else; we condemn ourselves to loneliness.

Let us admit our imperfections; they are part of our humanity.

*Geese lower their heads when flying under a bridge, no
matter how high its arches may be.*
                                —Julius Caesar Scaliger

Old fears oppress us. They can hamper our
growth; we learn nothing from them. Yet
many of us continue to be afraid, for reasons
we have long since forgotten, or never knew.
Our bodies sometimes carry the weight of
these old fears; a cringing of the shoulders or
a knot in the gut may be part of the legacy.

Our growth as free beings may depend on
shedding these old fears. They are as real as
viruses, and they make us ill in similar ways.
We need to examine our actions, to be sure
that we aren't just ducking our heads every
time we fly under a bridge. Am I behaving ap-
propriately? Am I meeting this situation in
this moment, or am I letting the past govern
me? Am I acting or reacting?

When we discard old fear, we have a sense
of liberation. Whatever wound that old fear
was protecting can heal. We are ready to face
life as it comes, not as we fear it might come.

*Healing myself empowers me to shed the fears
that limit my growth.*

Gentleness is not a quality exclusive to women.
                                        —Helen Reddy

Our options for how we respond to the men and women in our lives are vast. Being critical is one option open to us. Indifference and gentleness are others. The way we treat others reveals our own state of being. When we feel at peace, we generally respond peacefully to others. Conversely, when we feel worthless and full of self-doubt, we're likely to be sarcastic toward others. However, we can pull ourselves out of the self-imposed dungeon of despair. The method is this: In spite of personal feelings, be warm, kind, and gentle in every personal exchange with another, and your own dark mood is sure to be lifted.

Again we are confronted with the reality that we make our world. Our treatment of others treats ourselves simultaneously. Our friends and co-workers mirror the self we often think we're hiding away. A conscious decision will guarantee the happiness we long for when the decision is to be gentle, loving, and caring toward all the people in our lives.

Today I'll be as happy as I want to be.

Our greatest happiness does not depend on the condition of life in which chance has placed us, but is always the result of a good conscience, good health, occupation, and freedom in all just pursuits.

—Thomas Jefferson

Opportunities abound each day of our lives for respectful, thoughtful actions toward others. It's within our power to apply serious effort to any task securing our attention. Being concerned with our physical health and emotional well-being is also a choice. And we discover the level of happiness we attain in this life is in proportion to the considerate attention we give to others, to our personal needs, and to the activities occupying us.

The blessings we receive in this life are measurable by those we bestow upon the lives of those with whom we're traveling. There really are no surprises in store for us. We each must assume responsibility for our own happiness and good fortune; and there's no time like the present for opening our minds to this reality.

We sit at the controls today, and our perspective on the situations we experience will make them pleasant, productive, or problematic.

The choice is my own. I'll find happiness and good will if I foster it.

If love does not know how to give and take without restrictions, it is not love, but a transaction.
—Emma Goldman

Many people form primary relationships before they've had a chance to live alone, to be on their own, to test themselves out in the world. Sometimes, in fact, it's fear of testing themselves that drives them prematurely into a relationship. So a lot of early relationships dissolve. And if the people involved in them are motivated by fear, they're likely to form new relationships before they've given themselves a chance to heal or grow from the old ones.

In a healthy relationship, both partners give and take without restrictions. Love is a process, an unfolding intimacy between adults. It's no substitute for a mortgage or a Band-Aid. It's difficult to conduct this kind of relationship when we're young and unsure. We need an enormous amount of trust to be nurturing and vulnerable. After we've knocked around in the world a bit, we're more likely to have the strength to form a real love bond.

Today I'll remember to promise only what I can give freely.

August 25

. . . the greater part of our happiness or misery depends on our dispositions and not on our circumstances.
— Martha Washington

A light heart eases a hard struggle. A sense of humor takes the sting out of troubling circumstances. Likewise, a hateful attitude takes the luster out of the brightest moments. We have the power to control the flavor of the circumstances which will invite our involvement.

Accepting responsibility for our own happiness frees us from others' control. And it heightens our moments of pleasure. We are in control of the level of our joy and sorrow. In any situation we may choose to give others control over our feelings, but making that choice guarantees that we'll live half-lives with little real happiness.

Knowing that happiness is always within reach if I extend my hand for it strengthens my grasp. I'll practice taking charge of my own happiness today.

Life is terribly deficient in form. Its catastrophes happen in the wrong way and to the wrong people.
—Oscar Wilde

Villains get punished and heroes triumph in well-made plays and books. In life it's not easy to say who's who; most of us are heroic sometimes and villainous other times. Our lives are an uneven mixture of triumph, reward, and hanging-in. Unjust events happen: children die, airplanes crash, rivers flood. The world contains starvation and abundance, violence and gentleness, in its pattern.

The strands of right and wrong, good and bad, are mingled; there's no untangling them. What contributes to our personal progress is our ability to accept this bewildering complexity. To live wholeheartedly, yet to detach ourselves from the outcomes of our actions is the secret of serenity.

When a catastrophe strikes, we may be unable to turn it over, to find any good in it. We don't know all there is to know; we see only a part of the world's pattern. Hanging on to a disaster multiplies its effects. We must feel our feelings and let them go.

I will work for surrender and acceptance; the days to come will hold brand new possibilities.

August 27

Every time a man unburdens his heart to a stranger he reaffirms the love that unites humanity.
—Germaine Greer

Intimacy is the gift that bonds us to one another. We understand our likenesses and can acknowledge our differences in this process of sharing ourselves. We can see how similar our fears and our hurts are, and in seeing we gain strength.

Becoming intimate with someone else unites us, enlarges our capacities to nurture the people in our lives. Our emotional growth is proportionate to our attempts at intimacy.

Too often we hold back from telling others who we really are, fearing that they'll think less of us if they know the person we hide within. Only the experience of self-revelation can assure us that others won't think less of us. Our unity with another is possible only if we share the person who lives within.

I must find unity with others if I am to have the strength to withstand whatever befalls me. The people around me can be trusted with knowledge of my inner self. I'll reach out today.

*. . . to have a crisis, and act upon it, is one thing. To dwell
in perpetual crisis is another.*
—Barbara Grizzuti Harrison

Misery is an option available to us every day,
over any situation. We can linger, befriending
despair. It is also possible to take life's rough
currents in stride, responding to them sanely,
thoughtfully, trustingly. The rough times, we
can see in retrospect, teach us the most.

Crises become too familiar to some of us.
They push us into overdrive and an elation accompanies them, an elation born from the energy inherent in the crisis. However, this same
energy is inherent in calm, sensible responses
to life if we'd learn to cultivate it. Crises ultimately burn us out, while measured, balanced
responses to turmoil rekindle belief in ourselves, and our ability to handle the gravest
conditions.

Dwelling in crisis allows us to avoid forward
movement. However, if we want to grow and
find the real happiness we deserve, we must
move ahead to the challenges that promise us
our due.

*A crisis may protect me from unknown oppor-
tunities today. It will also prevent growth. My
choice is open.*

We do not weary of eating and sleeping every day, for hunger and sleepiness recur. Without that we should weary of them. So, without the hunger for spiritual things, we weary of them.

—Blaise Pascal

A great spiritual hunger is a hallmark of our age. Our age, however, is such a secular one that many of us do not recognize this hunger for what it is. We feel an emptiness and we try to fill it with consumer goods or exercise workshops. Our restless narcissism takes up one fad after another but, since we were not truly hungry for them, we weary of them.

Spiritual nourishment comes only with self-forgetfulness. This seems paradoxical; and yet transcending ourselves is the greatest gift that can be bestowed. Haven't we noticed that the people who seem most at peace in the world are those who live for others?

When we find a true source of spiritual wealth, we can learn to satisfy our hunger. And it will recur! Our needs for refreshment of the spirit will be more focused, better defined, and we will know how to satisfy them. We can never nourish our spirits by concentrating on ourselves.

I will strengthen my spirit by endeavoring to achieve selflessness in my dealings with others.

*Don't do nothing you can't share, and be prepared to discuss
everything that you do.*
> —Martin Shepard, M.D.

Secrets diminish self-respect; they foster para-
noia, and they make it impossible to have honest and open communication. Self-disclosure
cleanses us; but an even greater benefit is that
a commitment to it triggers careful forethought, and a needless or perhaps hurtful action can be avoided.

It takes only a moment to reflect on the
possible ramifications of an intended action.
And that moment's reflection can save us from
apologies, shame, and embarrassment. Being
committed and prepared to inform others of
all that we are nurtures the growth of our better selves. No greater encouragement for self-
improvement exists than the decision to share
absolutely all.

*I will think before acting today and find free-
dom from shame.*

August 31

The reward of labour is life.

—William Morris

Almost everyone complains about work: the price of fertilizer, the drudgery of housework, the bureaucratic details, and the long hours. Whether we're mechanics or physicians or keypunch operators, most of us complain about the work we do.

Yet without work, where would we be? How could we derive a sense of ourselves as connected to the world if we weren't involved in it through our work? Work is the fiber of our lives. It nourishes us and provides us with a measure of ourselves. When we're productive, we feel good. When work loses its meaning, we feel bad.

We owe it to ourselves to find work that fulfills us. We need the rhythm of tasks begun and completed for our spiritual health. When our work violates us, we suffer. Then we need to look for creative solutions to end our pain—changing the work we do, taking risks.

Work is our blessing. Today I'll be grateful for good work; what I do, I'll do well.

September

September 1

What is this life if, full of care,
We have no time to stand and stare?
                    —William Henry Davies

Souls, like animals and plants, need air. Do our lives have enough empty space in them to nourish our spirit? Living in cities, plugged into networks of jobs, friends, and projects, we sometimes neglect our standing-and-staring needs.

They're quite specific: we need to be outside, in pleasant weather, with nothing much to do. We need to let the world go on its way without us for a while. We need to have things pass before our eyes: clouds, or boats, or waving grass.

Blessed idleness! Blessed inattention! When we slip back into the groove, we're refreshed by our passive interlude. Let's remember the recipe and find some time to stand aside and stare.

If I don't take the time, it will take me. I'd rather the choice was mine.

I believed what I was told and not what my own eyes saw.
—Margaret Drabble

Children see a flat world and are told it is round. We are trained very early to disbelieve the evidence of our senses. But there comes a point when we begin to question what we are told and to feel that our own vision is probably as keen as anyone's.

Independence of thought can be an admirable quality. It's also a quality that distinguishes those we call crackpots. Where do we draw the line?

It's important always to try to disentangle what we want to believe from the evidence of our senses. Wanting events to have a certain outcome can blur our view of what is actually happening. We can delude ourselves to the point of denying the reality we perceive in favor of some ideal, some fantasy.

Testing our beliefs against what our own eyes see and the opinions of those we respect will keep us balanced between skepticism and delusion. Life is rich and baffling enough without our fantasies to complicate it.

My uncorrected vision sometimes distorts my reality.

September 3

The great thing in this world is not so much where we are, but in what direction we are moving.
—Oliver Wendell Holmes

We may feel idle, but we are not. We are moving along some pathway at every moment, and each of us needs to accept responsibility for our movement and determine our course. For when we are not moving forward toward our desired destination, we are moving away from it. We are moving, always.

Having a goal inspires concrete action. It fosters planned movement, a focus for the day. Additionally, it facilitates decision making. Living without goals diminishes the joy that's inherent when we respond advantageously to an inviting opportunity. Further, we can only truly recognize essential opportunities when we are in command of our direction.

It may be difficult to look forward to the days ahead if we have no dream to shoot for. Perhaps a goal for some of us is simply to choose a goal.

I never stand still. I will take charge today of the movement that's guaranteed. I will go where I want to go.

It is only when there is nothing but praise that life loses its charm, and I begin to wonder what I should do about it.
—Vijaya Lakshmi Pandit

We lose our appreciation for joyful times when they become a matter of course. Compliments lose their delicious quality with overuse. Balance in all things offers the greatest satisfaction.

It's not likely that we realize the full value of variety in our lives. Probably we long for easy times, the absence of struggle, and certainty regarding outcomes. Were life to treat us in such manner, we'd soon lose our zest for the day ahead. The sense of accomplishment that we hunger for is nestled within the day's rough ripples.

Our experience in this life is purposeful, which means there are matters we'll be asked to attend to. Not every involvement will provide pleasure. Some, in fact, will inflict pain, but we'll discover elements that will enhance our self-awareness. Through this knowledge we'll find lasting fulfillment.

Today will be a mixture of joy, boredom, perhaps both pain and sorrow. Each element will give me reason for growth.

September 5

I accept life unconditionally. . . . Most people ask for happiness on condition. Happiness can only be felt if you don't set any condition.

—Arthur Rubinstein

When life offers you lemons, make lemonade, so the saying goes. It's simple and true. No matter the circumstances of our lives, we can maximize the positive events. More importantly, we can learn from the negative ones. In reflections on the past, we are frequently surprised to discover that the lemon made possible the deliciousness of a present experience.

All events of our lives are threads, weaving a pattern that is unfolding by design. Each experience is equal to every other experience. We shouldn't cling to any one of them, or shrink from any. It's their sum that makes us who we are. Each of us is a mosaic unto ourselves. And yet, by design, our patterns, our lives intersect.

An expectation that an experience is a necessary part of our design will foster gratitude, even in the moment that we must swallow the bitter fruit.

Today I'll be faced with some lemons. Can I make lemonade?

A depressing and difficult passage has prefaced every new page I have turned in life.
                                            —Charlotte Brontë

What would it be like to shed our old skin, like a snake, when it grew too small? Perhaps the discomfort we feel at each new stage of growth is something like that feeling. Truly, each new page or stage of life has a difficult introduction—but if we can only remember that, it may help us through the bad times.

Too often, in the grip of change, we lose sight of what we are becoming. Did you ever wonder how it would feel to be a grub and then turn into a winged creature? It helps us to endure the depressing passage if we can remember that we're being prepared for a new stage of our lives, one in which, perhaps, we will leave our old selves as far behind as the dragonfly leaves the larva.

With time and wisdom comes the knowledge that some pain always accompanies growth. We can accept the pain more gracefully if we remind ourselves that we are preparing to turn a new page.

My spirit, like my body, holds the secrets of growth and change.

September 7

Tomorrow doesn't matter for I have lived today.
—Horace

The twenty-four hours lying ahead is all we have been promised. With that promise is a guarantee that we will greet opportunities for growth that have their roots in yesterday. Our evolution is not without purpose and design; therefore, we need not concern ourselves with the future. It will educate and comfort us as it becomes the present.

When we understand that the situations inviting our responses today have purpose, our anxiety is eased. Fear is allayed when our understanding is complete. Our life experiences are not happenstance, of this we can be sure; there exists an interdependence. Events are woven together for our greater good. Moreover, no one event offers more than a glance at the whole picture. So what we see today enlightens us about yesterday and last week, even last year, perhaps. Tomorrow will do likewise. But today is our only concern. It will provide exactly those opportunities we need to weave the next portion of our chosen design.

I am peaceful. Today will take care of my needs.

*To dream what one dreams is neither wise nor foolish,
successful nor unsuccessful. No precautions can be taken
against it, except, perhaps, that of remaining permanently
awake.*

—Margaret MacDonald

Dreams, like desires and feelings, simply happen. They happen to everyone from early
childhood to old age; they're part of the life of
the human mind, and we can't really control
them. All we ever can control is our behavior—how we act on our dreams, our desires,
and our feelings.

At times some of us try to control the un-
controllable, and stay "permanently awake,"
to fence out or repress the sadness, desire, or
rage that we don't want to feel. By doing this,
we make ourselves doubly unhappy; for human beings are creatures of feeling and fum-
bling. To try to engineer the unruly parts out
of our lives is just to create another way to feel
bad, for the attempt is doomed to fail.

Accepting our roughness, the violence and
vulnerability that live within us, is to let go of
shame. Why be ashamed? All others are the
same as we. We can't choose our feelings, but
we can choose how—or whether—we express
them.

*If I fence out my dreams and feelings, I turn
them into enemies.*

When we cling to pain we end up punishing ourselves.
—Leo F. Buscaglia

Painful situations, relationships that hurt us, memories of experiences that pinch our nerve endings, need not imprison us. However, we are seldom very quick to let go of the pain. Instead, we become obsessed with it, the precipitating circumstances, and the longed-for, but often missed outcome. We choose to wallow in the pain, rather than learn from it. And we salt our own wounds every time we indulge the desire to replay the circumstances that triggered the pain.

Pain can't be avoided. It's as natural as joy. In fact, we understand joy in contrast to the experiences of pain. Each offers breadth to our lives. And both strengthen us. Our maturity is proportionate to our acceptance of all experiences. In retrospect we can be grateful for pain, for it offered us many gifts in disguise.

I can see pain as part of a bigger picture, if I so desire.

I was tender and often, true;
Ever a prey to coincidence,
Always I knew the consequence;
Always saw what the end would be.
We're as Nature made us—hence
I loved them until they loved me.

—Dorothy Parker

Did Nature really make us so that we despise those who love us? Groucho Marx's joke, "I wouldn't belong to any club that would have me for a member," implies the same thing. But this can't be; we're children of the universe, each of us exactly as lovable and fallible as all the others.

Many of us go through years of upheaval in which we want only what we can't get. If we should get it, heaven forbid, it turns to rubbish in our hands. Some people call this the "reverse Midas touch," and it's common enough so that we all recognize it.

This is a symptom of self-mistrust, of self-dislike. If we believe in ourselves, we'll evaluate those who are drawn to us on their merits. For someone to love us doesn't automatically mean that they're deluded. It might simply mean that they love us.

If I don't love and value myself, I won't really be able to love back someone who does.

September 11

We saw endurance, chance, and law. We knew transience but glimpsed eternity. We learned that nature's flux is constancy and we were at ease.
                    —Edna Hong and Howard Hong

Precious are the glimpses we get into the nature of things. But we must be ready for them, or the most exquisite lessons will be lost on us. Anxiety, regret, or egotism can cloud our perceptions. We only learn when we can set aside our preoccupations.

To be hung-up is to be caught, like a coat on a hook, unfree. When we're hung-up, our attention is somewhere else; we can't learn anything. And hang-ups are a choice we make. If we choose the freedom to experience nature's flux, we can slip off the hook.

Mainly we choose to stay hung-up out of fear—fear of the unknown and perhaps fear of freedom. If we've spent most of our lives on one hook or another, we may not have much confidence that we can get along by ourselves. But we can.

Today I'll choose freedom and groundedness. I'll choose to learn ease.

The change of one simple behavior can affect other behaviors and thus change many things.

—Jean Baer

The effects on every action are far-reaching. Our response to a particular set of circumstances will influence its outcome and the lives of all persons concerned. Harsh words one time, a smile and praise another, will make their mark in the system that includes us all. Our actions and interactions are interdependent, each one having been affected by preceding actions and in turn affecting those that follow.

A single action has impact on our subsequent actions. An angry retort is likely to influence our behavior toward the next unsuspecting person who gains our attention.

A grateful attitude expressed will soften the harsh realities of life for the giver as well as the receiver. The principle underlying all behavior is that it breeds itself repeatedly. Positive, respectful action can become habitual.

Let me remember that I'm creating habits by my every action today. I can make them good ones as easily as bad ones.

September 13

To live is not merely to breathe, it is to act; it is to make use of our organs, senses, faculties, of all those parts of ourselves which give us the feeling of existence.
—Jean-Jacques Rousseau

We are gifted with talents that need encouragement in order to blossom. Few of us fully appreciate our talents. Many of us fail to utilize them. And yet they are waiting for the invitation to present themselves.

We have been blessed with particular talents because the world we live in needs our individual involvement. Each of us is charged with a responsibility to contribute to the lives around us. Our shared talents make the road smooth, when each of us has acted as the need arose.

We are called to participate by our talents. They help define who we are. They affirm that we count, that we are needed. No one is without a capability, a characteristic that lends just the right flavor to a situation involving others. Whether it's a sense of humor, the ability to write or paint, or a talent for settling disputes, we each have a calling card, and we are asked, daily, to make our contribution.

Am I willing today to participate fully in the life around me?

Out of every crisis comes the chance to be reborn. . . .
—Nena O'Neill

It is not our smooth passages that reveal new understandings, but the strenuous, uphill battles that benefit us with the knowledge we need to grow. Looking on our challenges as gifts whose resolution promises greater comfort makes them agreeable, perhaps even prized. Without them we stagnate, and life's joys are few.

Life is a series of lessons. And our crises are our homework. The patience and the trust we developed while living through last week's crisis has prepared us for greater benefits from those that lie ahead. Knowing that a crisis guarantees us the growth we deserve makes its sting endurable.

Every crisis is followed by a time of easy stepping. These restful periods let us adjust to our new stage of development, and they invite us to store up our strength, our energy for the tests that lie ahead.

Every stage of an experience has its roots in the past and leans toward the future. I'll trust that whatever I encounter today I'm prepared for and will benefit from.

September 15

It is astounding . . . how much energy the body is capable of pouring out and then replenishing. That is a magical act, because you never really understand where all that energy comes from.

—Robert Bly

The energy and persistence of a motivated person are truly marvelous. The work that nourishes us, the work that is a form of rapture, a form of praise, is magical. Where does our energy come from? Surely not from breakfast cereal, sandwiches, or coffee. It is a magical transformation of earthly food into pure spirit.

Rapture isn't our daily state, but we can achieve it. We achieve this rapt state when we forget ourselves, when we're totally immersed in the work that transforms us—whether it's clearing a field, playing a cello, collecting stamps, factoring an equation, or kneading dough.

If we're lucky, we discover this capacity for transformation while we're young. Some of us spend our whole lives searching for it. Most of us come upon it somehow: the key to releasing our limitless energy of mind or body. Self-forgetfulness is basic to it. The strength of the spirit does the rest.

When energy flags, it's often because I'm preoccupied with self. To renew my energy, all I need do is get out of my own way.

We are not educated: most of us cannot read or write. But we are strong because we are close to the earth and we know what matters.

—Mie Amano

The important thing in life is to know what matters for us. Our reality and values are our own; no one else can dictate them to us. They come out of our experiences and observation, and our spiritual health asks that we be true to them.

Similarly, we must be true to what matters for us. We won't try to win anyone over. Nor will we let someone else sway us. We will respect each other's reality, for that's how we will live in peace.

Further, if we're open and frank with each other, and with everyone else, we can spread integrity, respect, and peace. Quakers have a saying, "Let it begin with me." Integrity will spread outward, in concentric rings, for we are connected with one another.

Strength and growth come from knowing ourselves, knowing what matters for us. If we respect each other, we will find the way to fit any apparent conflict into a broader system that can accommodate us both.

If I am honest with myself, I can be my own best teacher.

September 17

Things are in the saddle
And ride mankind.

—Ralph Waldo Emerson

Some of us buy expensive toys on impulse; tire of them quickly; and let ourselves feel hopeless and inadequate because the impulsive wish was a shallow one. To ease our pain, we buy new toys—and so it goes.

Each new thing we acquire means new responsibilities: insurance policies, computer software, installment payments, safe deposit boxes. Deadlines and taxes oppress us; we dream of "getting away from it all."

At some point, we chose everything in our lives. If we wish, we can choose to do without. When we feel suffocated by our possessions and obligations, it's good to clear our minds and think about what we really want. Many of us don't think about our values consciously until they become a source of pain.

We'd be kinder to ourselves if we were fully aware of our values when we make choices in our lives. Are we choosing things as a shortcut to happiness—or a substitute for it? If we feel an emptiness that we've tried to fill with things, we'd do better to tend our spirits.

Let me learn to trust myself; then I know I'll like what I do.

We are only as sick as the secrets we keep.
—Anonymous

Not letting others know who we really are keeps us continually off balance while in their presence. Risking full openness, even with friends, is not easy; however, the pain that accompanies secret-keeping far exceeds the potential pain of self-revelation.

There are unexpected gifts for our complete honesty. One is discovering that we're like others. We're not unique in our shame or our self-abhorrence. And the attachments to others inspired by our decision to share ourselves strengthen us. The pain of alienation diminishes. We begin to sense our equality, one with another, and we experience trust.

Sharing secrets, our own and others', lessens the burden of guilt that diminishes each of us. But more than that, our freedom from secrets nurtures healthy personal growth. Hiding nothing convinces us that we have nothing to hide; thus, we're free to try new behaviors, move in unfamiliar directions.

My burdens are only as heavy as the secrets I hang on to.

It isn't for the moment you are stuck that you need courage, but for the long uphill climb back to sanity and faith and security.

—Anne Morrow Lindbergh

It's not just major challenges that require courage. Even the minor skirmishes with life demand some deep breaths, perhaps hushed prayers, and lots of hope. We'd glide more easily through every day if we'd accept that struggle is part of the process of life; that it offers more opportunities for us to realize our individual potential than any other dimension of life.

Struggles strengthen us, enrich our character, temper our emotions. They enhance our being in untold ways, and yet we plead to be spared them. How ironic that we each long for greater success, at least some recognition for our accomplishments, but recoil from the very experiences that guarantee these personal satisfactions.

My struggles today are my gifts in disguise.
I will grow accordingly.

We succeed in enterprises which demand the positive qual-
ities we possess, but we excel in those which can also make
use of our defects.

—Alexis de Tocqueville

Those areas of our lives we struggle with the
most, such as impatience, control, energy, or
procrastination, offer us opportunities for
great victories. But even more, they offer
greater learning, and the greatest chance for
further growth and development when we relinquish our struggle. We can be certain that
any activity attracting our involvement will
provide chances to demonstrate both our positive qualities and our defects.

Our human need to be rid of defects can
hamper our progress, keeping us stuck in old
behavior. But when we've come to accept
defects as normal we can even capitalize on
them. They define who we are momentarily.
We need to remember that defects are generally assets that have become twisted with use.
Therefore, we can understand their origin and
smooth off the rough edges. Assets and defects
will switch places in our repertoire. We can
use each for the greater good of the enterprise
deserving our attention.

Defects have so much to teach us. They
offer us meaningful opportunities for growth
and mature action. Today's assets were yesterday's defects and where we stumble today, tomorrow we'll glide.

My defects will offer me new learning today
if I relinquish my incessant urge to be free of
them.

September 21

To expect life to be tailored to our specifications is to invite frustration.

—Anonymous

Life is what it is. It seldom matches our hopes and dreams, but it never fails to be exactly what we need. We are shortsighted, really. Reflections on the past can enlighten us to this fact. Seldom does any plan develop as we'd assumed.

Perhaps we are only beginning to realize that there exists a carefully orchestrated plan that each of us has been invited to experience. Our contributions help to form the plan which enhances our personal development. We are privy to the tiniest segment at any one moment, however. We must trust that the plan has our best interests at heart, even though our sights may be focused elsewhere. The evolution of our lives, often in spite of our own misguided efforts, should convince us that we can let go of the reins.

What life offers today is what I need—no matter what I may think!

*Speak your truth quietly and clearly; and listen to others,
even to the dull and the ignorant; they too have their story.*
> —Max Ehrmann

We have been invited to share ourselves in
this phenomenon called life. We are not fully
cognizant of the value of our gifts to one another. We don't know which words we mutter
might be the pearls of wisdom for another.
However, we can be certain that we'll show
the way to someone else. Each of us is acting
as a guide for another, perhaps a friend, perhaps an enemy. Whenever the student is ready,
a teacher will appear. We are all students. We
are all teachers.

How reassuring to know that we have a
story that counts in someone else's unfolding.
And it's equally exciting to contemplate how
another's progress will nurture our own. But
we need another's attention in order to be certain that our movements are in the right direction.

*I can't be certain whose story I need most to
hear today. I can only be attentive to them all.*

September 23

. . . we both want a joy of undeep and unabiding things . . .
— Gwendolyn Brooks

When I can live fully in each moment, I can open myself to beauties that might otherwise escape me entirely. The more attuned I am to what is really going on right now, which means unhooking my mind from preoccupation with the past and worry about the future, the freer I am to catch fleeting perceptions and subtle shifts in the world about me.

We know that we only use about 10 percent of our brain's capacity for the ordinary business of living, which includes building space shuttles and filing tax returns. The more fully we can bring all of ourselves to each moment, the more of our capacity is available for living.

Life isn't last year, or ten minutes from now; it's now, this moment, which will pass and be followed by more passing moments, a flow of time in which we're carried forward. Our journey is smoothed when we learn to let go, and it's eased by the joy we learn to take in "undeep and unabiding things."

Paradoxical but true: I'll find lasting happiness only when I let go of the notion of permanence.

Happiness is an endowment and not an acquisition.
It depends more upon temperament and disposition
than environment.

—John J. Ingalls

We carry within us the ingredient which assures smooth travel today, if that's our choice. In our exchanges with life, we can project an attitude of gladness or regret. We can be grateful for our blessings or resentful that we have only what we have. We can offer love to our fellow travelers or harbor envy. However, when we choose to enter a situation, a discussion perhaps, offering loving acceptance of whatever we encounter, we'll discover the prevailing inner happiness.

Becoming aware that the power to be happy is at our fingertips is profoundly exhilarating. At first it may also be frightening because we can no longer deny responsibility for our feelings. Every moment of our lives we are making a choice about how to feel.

Emotional maturity follows on the coattails of responsible choice-making. Never again must I wait for another to make me happy. It's in my power to be happy, today.

September 25

Old things were stirring: the old illness of remembering was going to start again.

—Rosamond Lehmann

Does the act of remembering ever resemble an illness? Yes, if it causes pain. For many of us, memories of our past behavior seem to live in cages, like wild animals; if we enter the cages, the beasts attack us.

Why do we give memory this power to wound? We sometimes seem to want the unproductive pain of a shameful remembrance, as though we had sentenced ourselves to feel badly, as if our pain could alter the past—or pay for it.

It's time to forgive ourselves. We know what's past is past, and the only time we have is the present. We may feel as though we carry a complicated weight of guilt and shame, but the act of releasing ourselves is simple—an act of self-acceptance. Let us greet the present in the best way we know, and let go of regrets.

I will tame my memories, so that they become my companions if I choose.

To love is to place our happiness in the happiness of another.
—G. W. von Leibnitz

Broadening our vision beyond our self-serving needs and acknowledging the importance of others in our lives not only lifts their spirits, but also fosters positive feelings within ourselves. Our personal happiness grows when we nourish someone else's.

That which we give to others will be given to us in time. In order to find peace, we must behave peacefully toward others. And to receive love, we must willingly and unconditionally offer it. When we try to control others' behavior, we meet resistance. We can be certain an aggressive stance invites adversity. How true is the axiom "we reap that which we sow."

My own behavior invites the treatment I'll receive today. I am free to act lovingly, respectfully, and peacefully.

September 27

But one of the attributes of love, like art, is to bring harmony and order out of chaos.

— Molly Haskell

The offer of love to the person sharing this time in our lives softens them, ourselves, and the events we share. Giving and receiving loving thoughts eases any momentary difficulty; loving and feeling loved reminds us that we are never alone in our struggles. In partnership we can survive any troubling circumstance.

Love of self, of family, of enemies, increases the harmonious conditions that affect us all. Like the ripples from a pebble dropped in a stream, the act of loving moves beyond the object receiving the love at this moment. In fact, the love we give is the love we'll receive.

It is a demonstrable fact that hatred breeds hatred. Just as absolute is the knowledge that the love we offer another makes easier their gift of love to yet another. Love multiplies itself and the harmony created nurtures us all.

Love makes partners of us all. No circumstances can fell me when I'm in company with another. I will look among my associates today for willing partners.

Honor: what a spiky, uncomfortable thing it can be.
I expect the young are wise to be dropping it.
                                        —Rose Macaulay

Each generation looks at its children with mingled pride and horror and thinks they are destroying standards, overturning values, and generally going to wrack and ruin. In Greece, in the fourth century B.C., Plato complained that young people had no morals and that their music was barbaric.

What we've not understood, for 2500 years and more, is that each new generation simply renames the old truths in the process of making them their own. Love, courage, honesty, generosity of the spirit—these values don't change, although they may turn up in unfamiliar shapes.

Virtues may seem spiky and uncomfortable to young people, who need to claim their own experience. But each generation will discover the truth for itself. We needn't fear that the new will destroy the old; it will simply make it new.

I will keep in mind that the young people of each age seek an identity that sets them apart from their elders—without realizing that in this way, too, they resemble them.

September 29

Even a happy life cannot be without a measure of darkness, and the word "happiness" would lose its meaning if it were not balanced by sadness.

—Carl Gustav Jung

Life is full of contrasts. What we perceive or feel at this moment is often heightened by an experience we just passed through. It's the sum and substance of all experiences and our feelings about them that give meaning to any single moment.

Joy is understood only in a life where discouragement has made its mark. Our lives are recharged, even glorified, by every moving experience, no matter what kind of emotion is evoked. In fact, our very existence is verified each time an encounter invites an emotional response.

When we are sad, it is because it satisfies a need to feel that way. If we accept this fact, our acceptance of every emotion grounds our lives in a serenity which embraces and transcends all our feelings.

Whatever I may feel today is cause for celebration. It's a sign of my vitality.

Mistakes are a fact of life.
It is the response to error that counts.
— Nikki Giovanni

We're not perfect. Our mistakes are consistent with the lessons we've been assigned to learn. We strive for perfection in ourselves and sometimes we demand it of others. And when we fall short of the mark, we frequently feel that all is lost. The most important and timely lesson any of us can learn today is that doing our best is as close to perfect as we need to get.

Since falling short of the mark is the norm among us, a second lesson is to learn to accept this fact. What counts is the effort. And even with our best efforts we can't be sure of the outcome. However, the outcome will be more satisfying if we are confident that we've done all we were able to do.

Shame over mistakes, or over shortcomings in general, is certain to exaggerate and multiply the negative self-opinions that generally haunt those of us who demand perfection. And the result is even more mistakes, because our attention is diverted from the task at hand. We must believe that mistakes are the guideposts to the destination we're headed for.

All is not lost if I err today. Mistakes help me stay on course, providing I'm willing to learn from them.

October

❧

October 1

Two birds fly past.
They are needed somewhere.

—Robert Bly

Our lives touch the lives of thousands of other people in ever-widening circles. Every act of ours has a public dimension, even something as private as sharpening a pencil or filling a teakettle. We all are needed by everyone, and our chosen lives become a necessary part of the larger pattern woven by all other lives.

Even by becoming a recluse or a hermit, we don't leave the pattern. We may change it, so that others direct their lives in a different way with respect to our own. But this is true of all choices.

And we don't see the pattern as a whole; it's too complex, too vast for us to grasp. About the best we can hope for is the optimistic detachment that lets us see that those birds are needed. The squirrels in our attic, the ants at the picnic, the angry driver honking behind us, are all needed. What can we learn from them?

Today I'll rejoice in my connectedness.

The sky changes every minute . . . on the plains side of the Divide most people have visions or go mad.
— Sandra Alcosser

Our adaptability is a constant source of amazement. We can learn to live and even thrive in such radically differing settings as a high-rise apartment in New York City and a sheepskin hut in Mongolia. We live in deserts, near swamps; on boats, in trees, and even underground. We can eat almost anything that any animal eats, and a lot of other things that no animal would touch. Our instinct for survival takes expression in our marvelous ability to adapt.

Some brain scientists believe that what we call madness is an adaptation, a technique for getting what we need. It's possible that visions are adaptive, too. Extraordinary behavior expresses extraordinary states of mind.

We're often hard on ourselves if we catch ourselves behaving oddly—humming aloud or weeping or staring in amazement at a spot on the wall. We want to be normal; we'll suppress the odd behavior. But we should pay attention; unusual behavior often means that something's going on inside us that needs attention. Maybe we're grieving a loss, or sitting on some anger. Self-acceptance and self-love will heal us better than scoldings.

I can accept even the unusual in myself. It is only one variety of humanness.

October 3

There is nothing so moving—not even acts of love or hate—as the discovery that one is not alone.
                                        —Robert Ardrey

We live in concert with others, compatibly at times and at other times not so well, but always with others. We don't always acknowledge our togetherness, but when we are moved to, we quickly sense the comforts of a shared journey. We belong to more than just our neighborhood, our families, our circle of friends. The concert that has captured us is greater, and it has a conductor with whom we travel a path as well. It's this journey that encourages us to appreciate the steps we take with others.

The whole of creation depends on the contribution of each part for its completion. Interdependently, never singly and alone, we exist. We are at one with another, and this oneness is eternal.

I may not feel our oneness today, but I will trust that it is so.

I search in these words and find nothing more than myself,
caught between the grapes and the thorns.
                                        —Anne Sexton

We are frequently afraid to look into ourselves,
to probe our depths. We've feared that if we
examined our basic motives and desires, we'd
find a swamp of evil: corrupt, selfish, and full
of hate. But we've learned—to our consider-
able relief—that those fears were unfounded.
We're human, that's all; not better or worse
than everyone else.

We all have particular traits that we struggle
with, parts of ourselves that make us unhappy.
When we're feeling down on ourselves, it may
seem that we're the only person in the world
with that fault. "Why am I so insecure?" "No
one else talks too loud!" "I hate being so competitive." If we could see into the hearts of our
friends and associates, we would find virtually
the same struggles.

And yet we go on fearing the monster lurk-
ing in those woods. Let's bring that specter
into the light; it's only ourselves, constant
traveler between pain and joy.

I only fear what I don't know; self-knowledge
is my real life's work.

October 5

My mission on earth is to recognize the void—inside and outside of me—and fill it.

          —Rabbi Menahem

Emptiness often haunts us. The alienation we feel that accompanies us to work, to parties, even among friends, is letting us know that we need to nurture our inner selves. Within each of us lives the small child who feels fear, fear about a particular outcome, or our ability to handle a situation. As we practice caring for our inner child in all of our experiences we'll discover a spiritual strength and a calmness that eluded us in the past. Consciously developing a connection to the inner child at first lessens the brunt of the external world, then removes it.

The spirit-child becomes our strength and our hope when we turn to it. It fills us; it comforts us as we comfort it. We no longer doubt our place in this life.

If I go within today to offer comfort, I'll find it. I will not feel alone or fearful if I reach within and take the hand of strength.

I was taught that the way of progress is neither swift nor easy.

> —Marie Curie

Some of our goals are easily attained. Others demand stamina and resourcefulness. And still others require a commitment of long standing, a willingness to postpone gratification, but most of all, an acceptance of possible failure. We can never be certain of a final outcome. We can only be sure of our effort. However, we can be assured that honest effort will allow us to make measurable progress.

Life is a process. We learn and grow and move toward our goals little by little. The choice to quit moving is also available to us. In fact, a breather from the path we're on is occasionally in order. Recommitment is necessary, however, to begin the growth process again.

Charging ahead takes energy—emotional, mental, spiritual, even physical energy. The whole person is involved in the process of growth; our progress is in direct correlation to the process.

Today may challenge me, but I will make progress.

October 7

The battle to keep up appearance unnecessarily, the mask—whatever name you give creeping perfectionism—robs us of our energies.

—Robin Worthington

Because we fear we're inadequate, and because our expectations of ourselves are inflated along with our assumptions about others' expectations of us, we live in the realm of pretense. However, the truth of existence is that we're exactly who we need to be. None of us is inadequate, yet all of us fall short of being perfect. Our journeys are designed to introduce us to new information, new possibilities for growth and development.

We must trust that we are at the right place, at the right time, with all the preparation we need to succeed, here and now. Fretting takes our focus away from the moment and the rich invitation for personal involvement that it's extending. Remember, it's through the full interaction with the present that we are nurtured emotionally and spiritually and encouraged to attain our full potential.

Today I'll remember that I'm all I need to be.

With nothing to do but expect the hour of setting off, the afternoon was long. . . .
> —Jane Austen

The most important single determinant of how we feel at any given time is our attitude. If we live in the moment, use the moment to the full, we will never be bored and seldom depressed. The surest way to bring on a negative mood is to deny the present, whether by dwelling on the past or by fantasizing about the future.

The past is unalterable; the future, beyond our control. All we have is now, and all we can work with is our present attitude and behavior. Everything that we value, our dreams, plans, and hopes, dwindle to insignificance before the moment. How we act right now is how we are right now. If we let ourselves dodge the moment, longing for a phone call that might not come or eating a candy bar because we'll diet tomorrow, we're negating all our best intentions.

I will look to the moment, and miraculously, the future will take care of itself. If I can achieve clarity and honesty right here, today, I'll give my future a good start.

October 9

We have our brush and colors—paint Paradise and in we go.

—Nikos Kazantzakis

We find in our experiences and in our daily reveries just what we anticipate. If we greet the day wearing a smile, confident that we are needed and able to make a contribution, we'll discover that the day holds great promise. What we need to understand is that every day holds just as much promise as we're capable of expecting. We carry within ourselves the image of the picture we're creating.

Since the choice to find happiness rather than sorrow and regret is our own, why does the latter even attract us? For no other reason than we fail to believe that we're deserving of happiness. We know our own shortcomings; we're aware of the details in our lives for which we feel shame. We think only the pure of heart deserve happiness. But we're human. And this means mistakes are normal and expected. With wisdom comes full understanding of this fact. In the meantime, we can trust that happiness is our birthright. All that's requested is our belief in it.

Today will offer me all that I truly desire. Happiness attracts itself.

Imagination has always had powers of resurrection that no science can match.

—Ingrid Bengis

Imagining the successful completion of a goal increases the likelihood of its attainment. Whether we imagine our success in an athletic event, a college program, or preparing a meal, the image formulates a mind-set that's conducive to the goal's completion.

Seeing ourselves leap with grace to hit a high, wide tennis shot makes the movement familiar when we're on the court. Hearing ourselves answer correctly a committee's queries reduces the anxiety when the test date arrives. Every anticipated event can be prepared for if we use our imagination creatively. However, we need to be aware that imagination can run wild if we're not responsibly in the driver's seat. At no time does someone else have the power to put wild, fearful ideas in our minds. And yet, we're each capable of absorbing someone else's negative suggestions if we're not actively imagining our own positive ones.

No day is free from some level of anxiety about an impending situation. Relief from this anxiety lies in my mind. I'll use my imagination wisely today.

October 11

Woe to him that is alone when he falleth, for he hath not another to help him up.

—Ecclesiastes

If we are stepping through this life, indifferent to those around us and thus separate from our fellow human beings, it is by conscious choice. It may be hard to reach out to someone close, but there will always be a willing hand to receive our own. Each of us has been created to offer others our unique gifts. When we choose a posture of indifference, we are denying to the universe what we have to give.

There is magic in the realization that our acquaintances, our co-workers and neighbors, are presented to us by design. We are here to learn lessons and we play teacher to each other. When we have stepped away from the circle of people calling to us, we are denying them the opportunities for growth they may need and preventing it in ourselves as well. We need one another, and being helped by someone else fulfills more needs than our own.

We are in one another's world by design. I will enjoy the magic of that meaning, today.

Nobody can hurt you but yourself. Every experience you have makes you all the more fit for life.
— "Box-Car Bertha"

We commonly say, "She hurt me," or "I'm afraid of hurting him." Yet no one can hurt us without our cooperation. Other people's actions don't affect us unless we choose to let them; and no words can wound unless we turn them into weapons.

Some of what we call hurt is really learning. Because our pride may stiffen us against change, especially when we're young, any learning that brings about a change in our behavior will hurt. As we learn humility, we bend more easily. And we learn not to accept pain from others.

All experience teaches us something, if we'll learn. There will be pain along with wisdom; perhaps the price of wisdom is pain. But everything we learn enhances our life.

I'll come to understand my pain and find its value for my life.

October 13

Every physician almost hath his favorite disease.
                                        —Henry Fielding

We wouldn't go to a dentist for corns or bunions, just as we wouldn't go looking for fresh fruit at a hardware store. By and large, we know where to go for what we want. Why is it, then, that sometimes we persist in asking something from one who cannot give it?

We recognize unreasonable demands when we meet them, but not always when we make them. Parents expect mature judgment from young children; children expect saintly patience or flexibility from their parents. Commonly, we expect our friends or lovers to show us their loyalty and affection without our asking.

Reality teaches us that if we want something, we should go to a likely source and ask for what we want. If we're not willing to ask, we'll have to settle for every physician's favorite treatment—whether or not we have the disease.

Today I'll remember to ask for what I want from an appropriate source.

Every human being has, like Socrates, an attendant spirit;
and wise are they who obey its signals.
—Lydia M. Child

At no instant are we honestly at a loss about
what steps to take, what decision to make.
Each of us is both guarded and guided by an
inner voice that we occasionally tune in on,
but more frequently tune out. We may have
defined the inner voice as conscience. However, it's not important what we think it is; it's
only important that we acknowledge it. The
inner voice is our special connection to the
spiritual realm, a network that links us all,
whether we acknowledge it or not.

The choice to listen to the inner message is
a ready option, and it will never fail to benefit
us. As we familiarize ourselves with it, and
trust it enough to act as directed, we'll glory
in both the comfort and the sureness of the
action we take. We sense that we're not alone.
Even when no other human is present, we're
not alone. Always we are connected to the
spirit-energy that inspires us all to right action.

Every dreaded circumstance is made easier if
I'm accustomed to going within for guidance.
Today can run as smoothly as I want. I'll seek
my inner voice.

No man is an island entire of itself. Each is a piece of the continent, a part of the main.

                                                    —John Donne

Our problems seem so singular; we often feel alone with our struggles. And it's true that each of us must come to our own terms with whatever situation faces us. But no struggle facing us is free from the influence of other people and their struggles. We have a shared destiny which is accompanied by individual perceptions and both singular and mutual responses to the ebb and flow enfolding us all.

Knowing that we share this journey offers comfort when we need it in our daily struggles. We are not alone, forgotten, unimportant to the destiny of others. Nor are others without meaning in the experiences we're gifted with. Our existences are mutual—we are interdependent contributors to the total life cycle.

What each of us learns eases the struggles of another. All experiences are meant for the good of us all.

Today I may feel alone, but I'm not. My life is fully in concert with those around me, and all is as it should be.

*. . . it wasn't sin that was born on the day when Eve picked
an apple: what was born on that day was a splendid virtue
called disobedience.*

—Oriana Fallaci

Liberty of conscience is precious to us. We
need to feel that we are doing the right thing;
sometimes, this may mean disobeying authority, as abolitionists, suffragists, and conscien-
tious objectors have done.

Yet when we search our hearts, it is our own
authority, or the authority of a spiritual source
outside ourselves, that commands our true loyalty. And others must trust this authority, for
themselves. Trust in ourselves teaches us to be
respectful of others' beliefs.

Obedience must be based on trust. If this is
true for us, we can understand that it's equally
true for others. Our spirit is larger than our
beliefs, and more generous.

*Today I'll try to understand that everyone
wishes to do what is right for themselves.*

Always I've found resisting temptation easier than yielding—it's more practical and requires no initiative.
                                        —Alice B. Toklas

If a temptation is easy to set aside, it can't tempt us very strongly. The real, insidious temptations are the ones to which we yield unthinkingly: temptations to inertia, for example, or to stinginess or self-punishment.

It's part of our puritan heritage that makes us equate "temptation" with "indulgence." We're armed against sensuous indulgence; we can be strong in resisting a casual romance, a piece of pecan pie, or an extra hour's sleep. We don't feel tempted by the small meannesses that nibble away at our souls, and therefore we yield without examining alternatives.

Can we learn to recognize these little temptations to anger, to a closed heart? Can we learn to see the feelings that we're tempted to suppress—feelings of love, pity, or communion with others—as occasions for spiritual growth and deliverance?

I needn't deprive myself of joy. Learning to recognize what tempts me to joylessness will help me to develop my spiritual wealth.

Some day science may have the existence of mankind in its power, and the human race [may] commit suicide by blowing up the world.

—Henry Adams

One hundred years ago, Henry Adams foresaw the plight we're in today. Some observers believe that people in positions of power won't be able to refrain from the awful destruction of a nuclear war.

If we believe that the glory of the human spirit is our ability to choose our future, it's important for us to refuse to agree. We must do everything we can to prevent this murderous suicide of our species, and the first thing we must do is to choose to leave war behind us. Our slow progress on this planet, from naked apes to technicians in clothing, has prepared us to make the noble choice of peace. We owe it to our humanity.

Among those who despair of our capacity to make this choice are people with brilliant intellects. They may not, however, be our wisest counselors. Each of us must listen to the truth within our hearts; there lies the wisdom that we need. Let's not confuse war with patriotism; we're all citizens of the whole world, and war hurts our human family.

When my spirit is tranquil, I can listen to the peace in my heart.

October 19

The evening star
is the most
beautiful of all stars.

—Sappho

The first star in the evening sky shines with a
special brightness, because it is the first. We
see it as a signal; the first sign that afternoon
has turned to evening.

The first of anything is touched with special
glamour; first love, a baby's first words or steps,
first day of school, first job. They're signals
of change, profound and irreversible. When
day turns to evening, that day will never come
again. Tomorrow is a new day, unique and
never-to-be-repeated.

If we could meet each new day, each new
person, each new experience, as though it
were the first, our lives could be touched by
the excitement and discovery of adventure.
We're not the same as we were yesterday.
Each moment we change; each new event in
our lives can be a cusp between two different
states. Today, let's give ourselves that special
gift.

Each moment is the first of a new series. I will
be attentive.

. . . What is in one's life stays there to the end of one's days.
—Harrison Salisbury

Young people often try to pretend they're
other than they truly are; they're pleased to be
taken for natives in a strange place, or tourists
at home. People try to change their hair color,
their body shape, or their voice—trying on
identities, escaping from themselves.

It's natural to play around with external signs
of who we are. We all look for a style that will
let us express who we want to be. But we're
indelibly marked by our genes and our up-
bringing. We're made so that virtually nothing
we've ever cared about is lost to us. Although
we can choose our behavior, we can't choose
our antecedents.

We may rail against this in our youth, but
by middle age, most of us will be glad for it.
One secret of happiness is liking who we are.
And that's where our power to choose is important: since we can't change who we are, we
gracefully choose to be the best possible us.

*I shall be grateful for this day, in which I can
make the most of what I have.*

October 21

Humor is such a strong weapon, such a strong answer.
                                        —Agnes Varda

We take life so seriously, certain that the situation confronting us, or at least the next one, will doom us. We gravely anticipate what lies ahead and assuredly we'll experience what we expect. The power to lighten our load rests within. We're only a decision away from an easier life, one that's built with laughter rather than perpetual gloom.

Few of us are aware of the therapeutic effects of laughter. As Norman Cousins demonstrated in his battle with illness, laughter can activate our total being, recharging the whole system. Besides the positive visceral effects, laughter grants a balanced perspective in life that encourages greater emotional health. Laughing at our human foibles takes away their sting, reducing them to minor irritants, the kind that are easily forgotten when we've developed a healthier perspective.

Nothing has power over us except by our consent. No problem, no difficult person, assumes command unless we've abdicated our own position of power. Remember the strength laughter lends us when a situation gets snarled.

Every situation has a humorous interpretation. My day will be lengthened if I look for reasons to laugh. Without fail, they are present.

*If you want knowledge, you must take part in the practice
of changing reality. If you want to know the taste of a pear,
you must change the pear by eating it yourself.*
                                        —Mao Tse-tung

Our language is poor in words that convey
emotional meaning. To know, for instance,
with the intellect, is not the same as knowing
with all our being. We can "know" in our
heads that the universe is infinite, but until we
experience that knowledge in our hearts, our
spirits, in the pit of our stomachs—we can't
really know it.

Full knowledge means change. Experience
of the infinite changes us; once we have experienced awe, we are not the same. We can understand oppression or injustice, but until we
experience it in our bones and breath, the
knowledge is not truly available to us.

The knowledge that changes is the knowledge we seek. And sometimes we must change
in order to obtain it. If we find ourselves living
in a way that contradicts what we know, we
change our lives.

We are continually changing as we grow.
Our spiritual progress is a record of small
changes that bring us closer to the truth our
spirit recognizes.

*I will not fear change; I will trust that it brings
the knowledge I need.*

October 23

To wait for someone else, or to expect someone else to make my life richer, or fuller, or more satisfying, puts me in a constant state of suspension.
—Kathleen Tierney Andrus

How tempting it is to make another person responsible for our happiness, and how absurd. To give such power to others means we're at their mercy; it does not mean we're happy. Whereas, accepting full responsibility for our own acts and feelings does give us the power to be as happy as we choose, as often as we choose.

Emotional maturity precludes our blaming or praising another for our personal well-being. There is reason to be exhilarated that we are blessed with as much control as we choose to have over our own growth, happiness, and commitment to change. We're in another's control only by choice—never by necessity. And when we've given our precious power away, we're reduced to waiting—waiting for someone else's nod of approval, waiting for their invitation to live.

The time is now to decide for myself who I am, where I'm going, and why! The time is now.

The true use of speech is not so much to express our wants as to conceal them.

—Oliver Goldsmith

Learning to communicate, for little children, means squeezing huge desires into little words, like "hurt" or "cookie." We learn early that we're only going to get part of what we want.

Some of us never recover from this disappointment. We use words to manipulate others, to hide our feelings. We may imagine that we have the power to control others, and so we tell ingenious stories to mask what we think is our naked strength.

But we're deluding ourselves, rather than other people. The strategy of falsehood and control finally traps us in a web of lies, where even we don't know what we want. Clarity is a choice, and so is happiness, if we want to choose them.

Asking for something is risky: I might be refused. But if I don't even ask, I'll never hear "yes."

October 25

The game of life is a game of boomerangs. Our thoughts, deeds, and words return to us sooner or later, with astounding accuracy.

—Florence Scovel Shinn

We plant the seeds of the bounty we'll reap by every action we take. We teach others how to treat us by our treatment of them coupled with our own level of self-respect. Never should we be surprised at the level of comfort or discomfort we experience in our interactions with others. We have invited it.

Fortunately, we are in control of our own behavior, which means we have the choice to act responsibly and with respect for others every moment of our lives. We can be certain that we'll be treated in similar fashion throughout the day. The terms of life are simple when defined in this way. We get what's our due—and we've prearranged it ourselves.

It's seldom that circumstances discourage us as much as our relations with others. Most often our frustrations or depression are people-centered. The good news is that we have the capability to favorably influence all outcomes that involve other persons. At every opportunity, remember the treatment we each desire and offer that to others.

I am in command of my behavior today. It will invite similar reaction. I'll put my best foot forward.

Though the seas threaten, they are merciful,
I have cursed them without cause.
                              —William Shakespeare

To each of us, our own self is the most important person in the world. I am the only person who can get what I want; you are the only person who can make you happy or unhappy. This doesn't mean that the world revolves around us, though.

When we were infants, we believed it did. We valued things according to how they affected us. A rainstorm was good if it meant we didn't have to visit relatives who bored us, but it was bad if it spoiled a picnic. We took everything personally.

It's not easy to give up being the center of the universe; some of us cling to the notion long after we've given up bottles and diapers. But once we acknowledge the impersonality of most events, we can stop taking responsibility for the weather, foreign policy, the outcome of labor negotiations. We can even stop taking other people's actions personally. Other people don't really get sick of us, succeed or fail for our benefit, or live or die because of us. It's wonderful to take the pressure off.

The only thing I need to take personally is my person.

October 27

The sun, the hero of every day, the impersonal old man that beams as brightly on death as on birth, came up every morning. . . .

—Zora Neale Hurston

Details bog us down. When we count the trees, we never breathe in the forest. Keeping our focus close means escaping the wider ranges of perception and robbing ourselves of the chance to see more than one little slice of life.

When we're children, everything is near and far at the same time. So many things are new that we need to anchor our perceptions with small bits of the familiar: security blankets, familiar toys, a well-loved thumb.

Grown-ups presumably learn to do without these "transitional objects." Yet we need some certainties in a life of shifting priorities and relative values. We're lucky if we can find our anchor within ourselves. We are the real heroes of every day; we come up every morning out of the individual details of our sleeping minds, and it's given to us to shine brightly on the events that touch us, whatever they may be.

Today may I find both zest in living and detachment from the petty details of life.

. . . my work was so long so little appreciated that I learned not to care a scrap for either blame or praise.
—James Murray

It's instructive to look at important figures of the past. So many have fallen into utter obscurity, and people who were quite obscure are now seen as important. Who remembers newspaper columnists or many best-selling writers of forty years ago? Yet at the time, their names were on everyone's lips.

We have an idea that life has speeded up, that history has accelerated, in that we live faster now than people did in the past. But this is a function of the media; the experiences we hear about are other people's experiences. We know more, sooner, about more people; we know when royal babies are born and when border wars are fought. But these events have always occurred, and have always totally engrossed those who are immediately concerned. Their true import for the world, history must discover.

When we have a staunch purpose, it's possible to ignore the praise or blame of those we don't care about. Whereas people who bloom early may be early sidetracked, the pace of our own lives is under our direction; so is our real significance in the lives of others.

Obscurity can be a blessing. It will never warp my values.

October 29

I think that most of us become self-critical as soon as we become self-conscious.

—Ellen Goodman

It seems all too common that we reject our own best efforts as not good enough. Few of us are satisfied with anything less than perfection in ourselves or others. Criticism is second nature to us, and it does an injustice to both giver and receiver.

The self-image of all humanity could stand a lift. Negativity has gained a strong foothold in our minds, and it digs its talons deeper with every barb given or received. Fortunately, we have the individual and collective power to change our thoughts and the direction we are heading, as individuals and in concert with others. Being positive toward ourselves and others wields great power. Positive strokes encourage greater efforts which guarantee positive results.

I can be self-critical or self-congratulating today. My choice will determine the day's success.

Who would care to question the ground of forgiveness or compassion?

—Joseph Conrad

Some people don't seem able to accept the things that come to them; they always want to go back and dwell on how it was before and what mistakes were made by them and others. Sometimes they want to prove, by this recital of past errors, that they were right; sometimes they seem to want to dwell on their own fallibility.

We can't make much progress toward serenity of the spirit without reconciling the past. If old wounds or conflicts rankle, we need to accept them, forgive them, and let them go. Above all, let's forgive ourselves. Those past errors turned into valuable lessons, didn't they? Life is too short to hold grudges, and they take up energy and time that we could use for spiritual growth.

Each day is new, and this new day is all of time for us, right now. This day can flow pure and clear or we can choke it with old grudges, regrets, or fears—the choice is ours.

The ground of forgiveness and compassion is fertile; from it comes my harvest of the future.

October 31

Adventure is something you seek for pleasure . . . but experience is what really happens to you in the long run; the truth that finally overtakes you.
— Katherine Anne Porter

In our search for new thrills, for unfamiliar ventures, we will become privy to situations and experiences designed for our personal growth. Our desires to chart new courses, to travel untrammeled paths, are consistent with the inner source of truth and knowledge that subtly and gracefully guide our movements.

Whatever the occurrences in our lives, the circumstances we'd rather shun as well as those that absorb us, we can relish the knowledge that they've sought us out to introduce us to new levels of truth. We can be secure that what we need to learn, we'll be taught. The experiences promising the opportunities needed to fulfill our personal potential will be present today and the days ahead.

I will trust today's experiences, secure in the knowledge that they are meant for me at this time.

November

�

November 1

Order is a lovely thing;
On disarray it lays its wing,
Teaching simplicity to sing.
                              —Anna Hempstead Branch

Things and events have their own order. It's human to want to impose order from the outside—our order; but often, our attempt to put things in order resembles the old man who tried to push the river. It never went any faster, and if he stopped pushing, it got there just the same.

Some people seem to have a knack for order. It could be that they've learned to let things take their own shape. If order is natural, then maybe disorder is what we create with our human fussing. It could be, too, that disorder is in the eye of the beholder—especially if the beholder is a perfectionist.

Serenity is the ability to appreciate natural order.

Today I'll try to be light on my feet and get out of my own way.

Putting a question correctly is one thing and finding the answer to it is something quite different.
—Anton Chekhov

Questions and answers lie within us. Unfortunately, they don't come in matched sets, numbered or color-keyed so we can match them up. Sometimes we think we have all the answers and we wish we knew the questions.

In fact, the questions are often more difficult to find, especially questions that have to do with our deepest feelings. What do we want? How do we feel about it? Such questions threaten to expose us—to lay bare our vulnerable selves.

For once we acknowledge that we want something, we risk not getting it. But if we can remain deaf even to question, we protect our vulnerability. The other side of that, of course, is that we'll never get what we want until we acknowledge that question. We must work to choose the risk of hearing the wrong answer over the certainty of deafness.

Is lack of pain worth shutting down my capacity for pleasure? Let me strengthen myself to risk joy.

November 3

Getting started can be very hard for people who have trouble with beginnings. After all, where do beginnings begin?
—Dorothy Bryant

Most of us have trouble getting started at one time or another. It's a common phenomenon, whether the project is Christmas cookies, an annual report, or cleaning the attic: "I just don't know where to begin."

It's a good rule to begin with ourselves, in the moment that is. Start the project where we are now. The other things that are necessary—details from the past and plans for the future—will reveal themselves as the project takes shape.

Sometimes we will begin, like writers, by talking about how hard it is to begin. This seems to oil the wheels; they start to turn, and before we know it, we've begun (though we may have to throw away the first paragraph).

Trying to begin at the beginning is a good way to drive myself mad. I will grasp the tools that are at hand: myself and the moment.

Together is a road travelled by the brave.
                              —George Betts

Moving through life fully in concert with others requires commitment and much energy. It demands self-love, unconditional acceptance of others, patience, the ability to be vulnerable and to take risks, and the decision to stay put even when the desire to run is great. And this assortment of characteristics is only the beginning. More is required of us, much more, if we want a real experience of belonging to those around us. But even more than that is guaranteed for us if we are willing to *be present always.*

If we've chosen to go it alone in the past, we can quickly recall the frequent uncertainty, the defensiveness when questioned by others, the absence of emotional support when the going was rough. But then, we may have believed we were free—others didn't have to be counted on. However, real freedom to be who we are can only be found among a circle of friends who have committed themselves to us, just as we've committed ourselves likewise.

Together we'll grow, find happiness, and gain strength.

I will lock arms today and move forward in the company of those who need me. I need them also.

November 5

We have a tradition in my family: We wash our own laundry, we raise our own children, and we clean up our own dirt.

—Alice Silverman

One life is all we have, and it's enough. One life contains plenty of joy, sorrow, exaltation, despair, astonishment, and cruelty. Why then do we borrow trouble? Every time we take responsibility for someone else's deeds, whether they're failures or successes, we're borrowing trouble—just as we rob ourselves when we refuse to take responsibility for our own.

Somehow we learn to give away our powers of independent choice. Somewhere we learned to say, "You make me miserable," and "Look what you made me do." But we can unlearn these twisted borrowings; we can learn to stand straight, be ourselves, and own our own lives. The power to be happy or miserable lies within us; when we give away our power to choose, we should be very sure we know what we're getting in return.

If I feel trapped, let me look at how I built the trap, and how I can take it apart. Where I used to say, "I can't," let me practice saying, "I won't."

The nature of consciousness is to flow. It seems ever changing. States of mind succeed one another. . . . We can direct consciousness to an idea or impulse, but we cannot lock it in place.

—Dr. George Weinberg

Our minds are marvelous, always moving, growing, absorbing, discarding, storing. And we are in control of the direction our minds take. Thus, it's by choice, either conscious or unconscious, that we dwell on negative outcomes rather than positive projections.

Claiming ownership of and responsibility for the direction of our minds and our lives develops a sense of individual power and, in turn, enhances self-esteem. *We are what we think.* We can think ourselves into becoming better selves.

We are free, at last, from the overwhelming feelings of powerlessness and impotence. The decision to take control of our thoughts and attitudes will be the turning point. When we complement that decision by offering positive direction to our minds, we'll quickly benefit from the advantageous outcomes.

I will utilize my personal power today. I will believe in positive outcomes. I will have hope.

November 7

There are two ways of spreading light: to be the candle or the mirror that receives it.
            —Edith Wharton

Each of us carries within us the power to illuminate others. Likewise, we are enlightened by others' gifts of perception. Every exchange of ideas, each expression of feeling, instructs us when our restraints against new information are broken down.

It is an awesome realization that whoever and whatever engage us are purposeful, having their place in our development at the moment. Nothing is for naught, and what we are inspired to share with another, too, fits into their scheme.

There is a message to be gleaned every moment. The choice to be enlightened awaits us.

Today will offer me lessons and information that I need. Will I accept enlightenment?

The most blessed thing in the world is to live by faith without imputation of guilt; having the kingdom within.
—Paul Goodman

What does it mean, to have the kingdom within? At those times when we're happiest, we also feel most blessed. The kingdom is one name for a peaceful spirit.

There are times, though, when we doubt whether anyone could live this way, in hope and joy. No regrets, no fears, no guilty conscience: how can it be? So often we feel we have to cover our happiness with misery, to feel bad in order to feel good. But the inner kingdom is built of self-acceptance. When we learn to love ourselves for the good people we are, that kingdom is ours.

Even when happiness is not our condition, even when sadness clouds our lives, we can be peaceful. By knowing ourselves to be good, and by believing we deserve goodness in return, we will acquire the strength to endure. The faith we live by is a peaceful, hopeful faith in the goodness of our spirit.

I'll work to free myself from the shadow of old shame and guilt. I can be as blessed as I choose to become.

November 9

*I was to give a child security and tenderness, but didn't feel
I received enough of this myself.*
—Liv Ullman

We can increase our level of serenity by learning to nurture ourselves. The child in us continues to need security and tenderness, even
while other children in our lives may call on
our reserves. We can ask for nurturing from
others, but our surest source is ourselves.

People who have never learned to love themselves may not be able to tap their source of
security and tenderness. It's never too late to
start loving ourselves, fortunately. Neglect and
abuse in early life may have damaged us; we
may have to unlearn many years of mistaken
lessons. What better time than the present?

Self-nurturing is a great adventure. We
must remember to have patience with ourselves, for deep trust and security, the kind we
all need, don't happen in a moment. Especially
if we're unlearning some damage, we must go
slowly. We are a precious gift, to ourselves and
others, and we deserve love and nurture.

*Today I will love myself, and patiently care for
my needs so that my security soon will grow to
include others.*

To be what we are, and to become what we are capable of becoming is the only end of life.
                                      —Robert Louis Stevenson

Our creation was our invitation to contribute that which is uniquely our own to the life process. Our brothers and sisters have been likewise invited. Our experiences are not without purpose. They offer us opportunities to practice the contributions we have been created to make.

Realizing potential is possible when we are committed to stepping forward to meet the challenges head on. No challenge is beyond our capability; every challenge promises new growth and a measure of serenity. Our search for security, for self-worth, if it's sincere, pledges us to stay with the daily challenges. They will teach us all that we are prepared to learn.

I go forth today with anticipation and gratitude for the opportunities to be wholly one. My experiences will be exactly what I'm ready for.

November 11

Miracles do not happen.

—Matthew Arnold

Many of us will insist that miracles *do* happen. We've seen transformations in ourselves or our loved ones that have seemed miraculous, strokes of fate, demonstrations of divine intervention.

Yet, we must do our part. If we look at the history of our personal miracles, we can usually see that time, pain, and patience prepared the way. Nothing comes from nothing. The changes that transform our lives are born from the suffering that is itself a reason for change.

Whether or not we believe that a higher power intervenes directly in this world's affairs, we realize, if we think about it, that humans must be ready. To catch a falling star, we must be standing under it.

Today I'll try to position myself in readiness for whatever miracle might come my way.

. . . the function of freedom is to free somebody else.
—Toni Morrison

We all struggle over the issue of freedom—
how much we want; how much we're comfortable with; how able we are to accept others'
freedom. We cannot grow and create unless
free to do so; in fact, our progress will be pro-
portional to the freedom we feel to breathe,
to move, to live fully.

   Control is the opposite of freedom. It steals
the freedom of the controller as well as the
one controlled. No one grows emotionally,
intellectually, or spiritually if energy is being
expended controlling. And yet, the human
condition is such that we passively, if not willingly, practice the game of control with the
many principal characters in our lives. It's a
game no one wins. Even when we're seemingly in control we lose our freedom, too, when
our attention is given over to the control of
someone else.

   No one is free until we are all free, and,
when free, we will find joy in our work, at
home, and with friends. We, too, will discover
the measure of joy we encourage others to
experience.

*If I reach out to love, I'll find love. If I mete out
control, I'll be diminished in turn.*

God's most lordly gift to man is decency of mind.
                                                            —Aeschylus

"Decent" means appropriate, proper, becoming. Decency of mind means to think appropriate thoughts, to respond properly to events and people, neither exaggerating nor trivializing their importance. What a consolation it must be to have a mind always in balance, always ready to dwell on the good and let the negative aspects go!

It's possible to achieve such decency. Perhaps it is a gift from a higher power; but we must ready ourselves to receive a gift like that. Becoming ready for the gift of a balanced outlook entails work: the work of overcoming our tendencies to, on the one hand, ignore, postpone, and forget unpleasantness, and on the other, to dwell on misfortune until we let it blot out the sun.

Decency is another name for the middle way, the true road. When we achieve decency of mind, we'll know it by the serenity of our outlook. Obstacles won't melt, but they will assume their true proportions.

Today I'll ready myself to receive the gift of a decent mind.

In soloing—as in other activities—it is far easier to start something than it is to finish it.
—Amelia Earhart

Our inspiration to master any art, to attain any goal, to tackle any project, comes from within—the center of all knowledge. All of us are gifted with all knowledge. When the desire to pursue a particular avenue keeps presenting itself, we should pay heed, trusting that we will be shown the way to succeed. This desire is our invitation to develop our talents in ways that may even be foreign to our conscious minds.

The decision to trust the desire is only the first step in tackling a new project. What comes after is effort and daily recommitment to completion of the goal or project. It is much easier to switch goals or projects than to see them to their end, but it's in their doing that we develop our talents to their fullest. Each time we back off, letting our commitment die, we are opting for less than a full life. No one else can handle a project in just our way.

Today I'll be faced with the choice to stay on top of my goals. I must remember the source of my inspiration and trust it.

November 15

To be happy means to be free, not from pain or fear, but from care or anxiety.

—W. H. Auden

The ancient meaning of "happy" comes from "hap," or chance—as in mis-hap, or hap-pen-ing. Happy meant fortunate or lucky, and we still call people happy who manage to turn life's unpredictability to their advantage.

Could happiness be a matter of attitude? If we persist in calling our cups half full instead of half empty, if we revalue setbacks as opportunities, aren't we behaving happily? Happiness of attitude is like a muscle: use strengthens it. Whatever *happens* to us, we should be determined to meet it positively.

Happiness can't protect us from life's woes, but it can ensure that we won't double those woes by worry or regret. We can't control other people or events; all we're responsible for is our own behavior. The decision to behave happily could change our life.

Anxiety shuts me in. I'll let it go and be free to respond happily to whatever comes.

Continuous effort—not strength or intelligence—is the key to unlocking our potential.

—Liane Cordes

Perseverance is the plus that assures us of goal completion. Unquestionably, every one of us is capable of achievement. All that's required is that we commit ourselves with determination to the task before us, one moment at a time, one day at a time. Our rewards will be many. Among them will be accomplished goals, high self-esteem, and a secure sense of well-being.

It's probable that we sometimes fail to recognize our worth or understand the real value of our talents. It's likely, too, that on occasion we shut out of our consciousness the knowledge that our very existence validates our necessity to the whole of creation. Self-reminders are important. They're like vitamins; they contribute to our nourishment.

When we have lost sight of our ability to make valuable contributions to society, we slow down our efforts. We close ourselves off from others and our potential is stifled. To move forward once again requires only our attention to the moment engulfing us. We can handle what lies before us.

Today my efforts are needed, in the here and now. That's all.

. . . be patient toward all that is unsolved in your heart and try to love the questions themselves like locked rooms and like books that are written in a very foreign tongue.
—Rainer Maria Rilke

We strive to know ourselves, yet we all have unsolved questions in our hearts. We don't need to answer them to achieve self-understanding; all we need do is accept them and understand ourselves as creatures with questioning hearts.

When we're ready to receive it, the answer will come within our grasp. Perhaps a lot of work will be required of us: as much as learning a foreign tongue. Or perhaps the answer will be as simple as a key that fits the door of a locked room. But no effort will get it until we're ready.

Patience seems like such a dull virtue, especially when we're young and eager for accomplishment. But patience is another name for love. If we're patient with ourselves, it's because we've achieved self-acceptance, and because we trust that, when we need it, the secret language and the locked room will be open to us.

I know I need not fear whatever lies hidden in my heart.

One is happy as the result of one's own efforts.
—George Sand

Our attitude about our circumstances or our
hopes determines the tenor of a moment,
eventually of the whole day.

No attitude, no feeling or emotion, is
foisted upon us. We have always made the
choice. Perhaps our passivity regarding
choices has all too often eased us into situations detrimental to our emotional health.
Nevertheless, responsibility for the pain that
accompanies poor choice is always our own.
Conversely, the joy that is ushered in by certain other choices is also our responsibility.

Personal power commands our lives, and
the fruits are as bountiful as are our choices,
selectively made. We will be as happy as our
choices make us, and as we decide to be.

*Today is all mine, and whatever I make of it is
by personal choice.*

When we are no longer children, we are already dead.
                    —Konstantin Brancusi

Children are born into a world whose rules they must learn. As part of the learning process, children always question rules. For simplicity's sake, we stop questioning most rules. We'll walk on sidewalks, eat with forks, talk in sentences, and keep our clothes buttoned. But the child inside us looks out with eager eyes and stands ready to question any rule that seems absurd.

Sometimes we bully that interior child into silence, for its questions embarrass us. Sometimes we hide it, sit on it, punish it—but it's always there. If we put that child to sleep, we lose one of the best parts of ourselves. We are right to question, to want to see for ourselves, especially when we're asked to do something that troubles our conscience. The child needn't always have its way, but it deserves our love. It was a young child in the crowd of people who said, "But the emperor is naked!"

I will love and nurture the child within me, and I will heed its questions, which may bring me to new answers.

Death, when it approaches, ought not to take one by surprise. It should be part of the full expectancy of life.
—Muriel Spark

The process of living includes many dimensions. We can joyfully anticipate high periods and we must expect pain. We won't escape sorrow over wrongs we've committed nor grief for the departure of a dear one. Anxiety over what may transpire is a given. But working to develop a balanced perception of all the events of our lives will ease our way. It's our overreactions to the ups and downs that make all of our daily steps uncertain.

Fearing the unknown wastes our time. How much better to trust that life will offer us exactly what we need to develop as healthy human beings. No event will be more than we can handle. All events are necessities of life, and each event needs simple acceptance.

If I understand that every situation carries a blessing, today will offer me comfort throughout.

November 21

Life is a battle in which we fall from wounds we receive in running away.

—William L. Sullivan

Our experience in this life is a composite of many lessons—lessons which will ease our personal growth and offer us the opportunities necessary to encourage our unique contributions. Clearly, not all lessons are easy or pleasurable when we first encounter them, but their rewards are great if we choose to learn from them, and we can be certain that no lesson is without its reward.

Those things we need to experience, to learn, to understand, will present themselves again and again until we have attended to them. We may choose to close our minds one time, and even close them again, but the lesson will not be put off for long. Another experience will surround us, offering once again the opportunity necessary for the personal growth we're destined to realize.

We must trust that our lives are unfolding in ways that will evoke our full potential, and that no challenge comes that earlier lessons haven't prepared us for.

Tackling my lessons head-on is a decision I can make today.

We cannot fail to meet the same problems as did our fore-
fathers, and learning their answers may help us to act upon
them as intelligently as they did, and may even, perhaps,
teach us to avoid making always the same mistakes.
　　　　　　　　　　　　　　　—Anne Fremantle

As youth, we are impatient and don't always
believe in the value of elders' experience. A
few mistakes, however, and most of us will acknowledge that we can learn something from
the wisdom of the past.

As parents, we want to protect our children
from suffering the same pain we have gone
through. We may have forgotten that some
risks are healthy. Fear teaches only more fear.
We must experience some failure and some
pain if we are to grow and learn.

The balance between safety and exploration
isn't easy to strike, but everyone needs to find
it. If we listen to the stillness within, we'll discover what is right for us to do—when to hang
on and when to let go. We will be able to trust
ourselves in both caution and bravery, and we
will learn from history all it can teach us. The
choices in our lives are ours to make.

If I am patient, I can understand and use the
experience of others.

A man that studieth revenge keeps his own wounds green.
— Francis Bacon

Our progress along the path of human growth is measurable by the exercise we encourage of our forgiving spirit. Each time we harbor a resentment toward another, we block our own growth.

Preoccupation with a troublesome situation or person prevents our responding to the thrill and possibilities of the moment. Stepping out of the flow of events to stay stuck on an old hurt guarantees us a stifled existence. Forgiveness of self and others frees us, frees our spirit to soar ahead. And we'll do so with a glad heart.

The act of forgiveness lightens whatever burden we may be carrying. Forgiveness heals the soul; it energizes the spirit. It makes possible our forward movement once again.

My hope for a good life is proportionate to my forgiving heart. Happiness is within my power.

Life is not always what one wants it to be, but to make the best of it as it is, is the only way of being happy.
—Jennie Jerome Churchill

The posture we take while performing our tasks today, and the attitude we project toward those who cross our path, will emphatically influence what the day brings. No one else can decide for any one of us what we'll feel or think about the day. We have the power to be as content or as discontent as we make up our minds to be.

A sign of maturity is acceptance of the full responsibility for the failures as well as the successes of a day. Another sign is the willingness to let go of the day's outcomes, whatever they are, and ready ourselves instead to face tomorrow, confident and hopeful. Carrying yesterday's baggage into today will only distort the size and shape of any bundle we must handle in the twenty-four hours ahead.

I begin the day free of yesterday, unburdened, hopeful, cheerful, confident, if I so choose.

November 25

Some people are so fond of ill-luck that they run halfway to meet it.

—Douglas William Jerrold

It's not wholly true in this world that we make our own luck, but we certainly have a share in it. Opportunity shakes out pretty evenly for most people, but what we do with it, whether we're willing or able to grasp a chance when we see one, is an individual matter. Some of us even have trouble seeing opportunities for growth.

When we feel abused or resentful, we need to examine our own part. Have we so mistrusted our own powers that we've not let ourselves see the chances life has dealt us? It's important for us to recognize that we have a choice. If we're dissatisfied, we can choose to change. We can also choose not to change, and to complain about being stuck; but we should realize the choice is our own.

If we've had a long string of bad luck, maybe we need to look at what we're doing. If our self-esteem is very low, we may want to punish ourselves somehow, to prove that we're no good. The knowledge that we're lovable and necessary people may have slipped away, and we may need to do some structural repair. But that's okay; we're worth the effort.

I deserve to be happy and I know how— whether I'm using the knowledge or not.

*It is not until our own hearts are pierced that we can begin
to know the suffering.*
> —Sarah Minturn Sedgewick

Our own painful experiences serve a worthy
purpose. They make possible our understanding of another's pain. In turn, we are able heal-
ers to one another because we have shared the
experience of pain.

Being present to another's sorrow or suffering is like a healing balm, lessening the burden, the intensity of pain. However, healing is
only possible after the pain has been acknowledged, internally embraced, and then released
by the injured person.

Frequently, we seek freedom from all pain.
But pain stretches us, pushes us to grow, to
develop new levels of ourselves. Pain promises
us unexpected pleasure. It also requires patience of us. We have many lessons to learn in
life, and each one is generally punctuated by a
stab of pain. It's within our power to rejoice
even when the pain is felt. It isn't without purpose.

*The pain I may experience today can teach me
and heal me, if I allow it to.*

Living well is the best revenge.

—Anonymous

Because we're human, and thus imperfect beings, we'll often be less than serene. In fact, tension and upset may commonly characterize us. However, the anger or resentment we too frequently feel toward others generally causes the greatest harm to our own lives. Although we may wish ill to others, it returns, like a boomerang, to ourselves.

We let others assume command over our lives when we give energy to our resentments. Those who are the objects of our focus gradually control all of our moves. We are no longer free to grow, to determine our actions, when we have given over our power to those we resent. Our attention goes toward them, and we forsake the steps toward our personal goals that need to be taken.

Wanting revenge is human, though always unproductive. We should understand, however, that those who have triggered our anger have garnered the greatest revenge. They've managed to pull us off course. It's up to us to take back our power and go about our lives with joy and direction. How much sweeter is this response to the ones who deserve our greatest consideration: ourselves.

Today I'll live well and productively; having a resentment is a choice that I never need to make.

It is only by forgetting yourself that you draw near to God.
—Henry David Thoreau

There is a spiritual presence which can aptly cushion our every fall, bringing comfort and subtle meaning to our lives. However, we'll not feel this gentle comfort unless we attune ourselves to the others in our company. It's within another's soul that we sense the beacon of light which illuminates the way we're traveling.

Broadening our vision so that we may see life from a stranger's perspective heightens the clarity of our own, and sharing the view bonds us, deepens all meaning, and closes the gap that lies between.

We must think and dream beyond ourselves if we are ever to sense the vast network that includes us all. We can be certain there is a rhythm to the unfolding of our experiences; a symphony which knows its own end.

Today I'll listen to the notes of others, and find my harmony with them.

If you have been put in your place long enough, you begin to act like the place.

—Randall Jarrell

Others can't put us in our place all by themselves; we have to go there. Our cooperation is required for snubs or for blame or for glorification. If we don't choose to accept the role another has found for us, we don't have to play it.

Sometimes it's difficult to accept the choices life offers us. It seems easier to go along with the roles that others assign. How many people do we know who seem to drift through important areas of their lives, neither fully cooperating nor asserting their own choices? They might not like to admit it, but in "going along," they've accepted someone else's definition of who they are.

Some of us comply out of a desire to cooperate—but there's a big difference. Compliance means refusing to exercise our own power to choose; cooperation means using our power together with others to achieve more than any of us can alone. If we accept the responsibility for our lives, we forego the luxury of saying, "Look what you made me do"; but in exchange we may get to do what we want.

I will remember that anything that happens between us is half mine and half yours.

He who does not start life well will finish badly, one can tell.

> —Great Calendar of 1500,
> quoted by Philippe Ariès

As a species, we're obsessed with the future. We spend time, energy, and money on horoscopes, almanacs, and sophisticated statistical "predictors," all of which, we think, will enable us to foretell the future. But life, economics, and the weather resist most of our efforts to control them.

In the case of children, predictions are more complicated. If a child's parents decide "this one's going to be a loser," that child has a lot of overcoming to do.

Can we escape the noose of a self-fulfilling prediction? Yes, probably. Health, self-respect, and a balanced outlook are easier to achieve for us if we have had loving nurturance and support in early life. But even if our early life has been filled with neglect or abuse, we can learn to love and nurture ourselves. And we can pass along the blessing by refusing to predict the future for others in ways that damage or confine them.

All we really have is here and now. All we can control is our own behavior. When we surrender to these limits on our human power, we can begin to tap the sources of a power greater than ourselves.

I will surrender to the moment today.

December

December 1

The still mind of the sage is a mirror of heaven and earth—the glass of all things.

—Chuang Tzu

In our own personal stillness, we find the solutions to the challenges facing us. We need to be willing to be quiet and turn our attention inward. No information we need eludes us for long when we dwell in the stillness.

Our opportunities for growth are hidden within the challenges that attract our attention. We need these if we are to contribute to the world. No challenge is beyond our capabilities or strength, and every one can be handled with relative ease if we have sought the comfort of the stillness.

The wisdom we admire in others is the birthright of us all. Each of us is a channel to full knowledge; any of us may be gifted with the wisdom to understand the present clearly, if we choose to exercise the commitment to move within ourselves—to the stillness, to the heart of all knowledge of the past, the present, and the future.

I'll have the answers I need, when I need them, if I turn within for them.

We should have much peace if we would not busy ourselves with the sayings and doings of others.
                                        —Thomas à Kempis

We can go forth peacefully today if we pay close attention to our inner urgings; they will direct our steps safely and justly. The choice is forever ours to respect this inner voice— rather than be nudged off course or have our progress severely hindered by the strength of another's self-serving tug.

Action that is clearly our own, rather than reaction to another's laments, is certain to bring personal satisfaction. This will strengthen even more the connection between the self we offer to the world and the voice that nurtures, guides, and safeguards us from within.

With practice we will develop an appreciation for all the people in our lives, and yet be free of their influence when it's not complementary to our own efforts. Taking full responsibility for who we are and where we're going is exhilarating. But even more, it's the only way we're certain of arriving at our most meaningful destination.

I will listen to and respect the men and women I meet today, but I will be most attentive to the friend within.

December 3

The first element of greatness is fundamental humbleness.
                                        —Margot Asquith

Recognition of the magnitude of creation heightens our awareness of the small but essential contribution that we each offer to the whole. We come to know that we are necessary to *its* completion, thus we are special. With that knowledge we are quieted, softened, and secure. We are at peace.

Sensing the meaning of our own existence enlightens us about others' value as well. This knowledge fosters love, respect, and acceptance of another's unique personhood. Each attempt at nurturing another is, in turn, an act of self-nurture.

The road stretching before us looks long and will often be rocky. We'll inch along at times. But when we remember our value, our unique necessity to the whole, the rocks will easily be sidestepped and our pace will quicken.

I will breathe deeply the realization of my meaning today. I am needed by the people I meet. And I will recognize their value to me.

We are a feelingless people. If we could really feel, the pain would be so great that we would stop all the suffering.
—Julian Beck

Other people's suffering is painful to us, but we have skins that protect us from the continual awareness of pain. We know that we are connected to all other life forms on the planet; yet we are distinct beings who can disregard the suffering of the torture victim, the slaughtered animal, or the starving child.

The thickness of our skins is good in one sense; it lets some of us be whole and happy in a world where many are not. But if it is too thick, we become callous. We shut out reality and pretend—successfully, sometimes—that everyone is as well off as we are.

It's difficult to respond to the suffering of others in a balanced way. The Serenity Prayer can show us how:

Grant me the serenity
To accept the things I cannot change,
Courage to change the things I can,
And wisdom to know the difference.

Much suffering can be lightened. Many decide to work, in some way, for the welfare of others. Our "feelinglessness" is only as deep as we decide.

My skin is a membrane that receives information from both sides. I will pay attention to both kinds of messages today.

December 5

At every step the child should be allowed to meet the real experiences of life: the thorns should never be plucked from the roses.

—Ellen Key

Reality is not always pleasant. More often it's painful. Accepting that pain, as well as pleasure, is part of the process of growth evens our responses to their presence in our daily lives. Being shielded or shielding another from pain directly hinders the rapture of pleasure.

Maturity is measurable by our response to the ebb and flow of the day, the season, even our lifetime. The vibrancy of life lies in the truth of experience. Myriad opportunities for growth, for rapture, for pensive meditation will present themselves every day. Absorbing from every experience will strengthen our character and prepare us for whatever lies ahead.

We cannot hide from pain. And we can grow from pain, whenever it appears.

Today may offer me pleasure and also pain. I need experiences of both to meet tomorrow.

*Women who have reached positions of prominence . . . have
not always been the best supporters of new measures to encourage female activism.*
> —Anna Coote and Beatrix Campbell

Generosity is a problem for some; they feel resentful. Giving to others seems unfair to them:
"Nobody gave anything to me," they'll say. "I
had to fight for everything I got." As if that
were a reason to deny others.

Giving to others takes nothing away from
us; on the contrary, it refreshes the soul. Yet
the fear that someone else's success will mean
our failure can keep us resentful and competitive.

Competition is drummed into us as children. It's a hard lesson to unlearn. But there
aren't many traits that are so unsuitable—and
so frustrating—as cutthroat competition. The
person who must compete is doomed to unhappiness and to a sense of inadequacy. We'll
stop the hopeless attempt to best others only
when we achieve the serenity of knowing that
each of us is the best at one thing: being ourselves.

*Being the best me I can often involves my help-
ing others.*

December 7

Every worthwhile accomplishment, big or little, has its stages of drudgery and triumph; a beginning, a struggle, and a victory.

—Anonymous

Every goal that offers us pleasure on completion has triggered periods of pain. The lessons we need to learn are seldom simple. Nonetheless, our development has relied on successfully tackling them. We can be certain that goals we are inspired to set for ourselves are tied closely to the lessons we're in this life to learn.

It's not unusual for us to want an easier life, one free from turmoil and pain. We'd rather not know that a life with no bumps falls short of the fulfillment we desire. But it does. We need struggles to stretch our capabilities.We need sorrow to appreciate the laughter. We need boredom to discover joy in small blessings.

Every worthy task will avail us of opportunities to grow, to think new thoughts, and to hone the skills we already possess. Every worthy task is destined to clear new ground for us.

Today I can celebrate, I'm on the road to victory. Every step leads toward the goal I've chosen.

Alienation is essentially experiencing the world and oneself passively, receptively, as the subject separated from the object.
—Erich Fromm

The goal of our spiritual quest is to put ourselves back together, reintegrating the self that acts and the self that observes. To be split is to be in pain. We feel our inner separation as a wound, and we try to dull our pain with frantic or self-destructive methods.

The pain won't yield to pleasure nor to danger or violence. These sensational methods leave us as alienated as we were before. We seek wholeness, and we'll achieve it only by surrendering to our sense of a reality beyond ourselves. Whatever we choose to call the great oneness, we must acknowledge it as a higher power or we'll continue to suffer the anguish of alienation.

Achieving serenity is a lifelong process. While we have this goal in view, our efforts will be unified and our attention not easily distracted by setbacks.

Today I'll resolve to focus on my spiritual goal and let it heal me.

December 9

When you hold resentment toward another, you are bound to that person or condition by an emotional link that is stronger than steel.

—Catherine Ponder

Our attention is consumed by what we want to control. Like a magnet, we are attracted to it; preoccupation sets in, and our freedom to live in the moment is gone. We give up living when we try to control others.

Our resentments grow out of our failure to control others, a failure that heightens our personal insecurities. When we need others to fall into line, to buy our plan, we have set ourselves up for failure. We have guaranteed that we'll experience the feelings of inadequacy that we dread.

Each one of us is on a path that is landscaped according to our inner needs. Accepting that will relieve us of the anger triggered when other people behave according to their own dictates rather than ours.

Resentment stifles us. To respond creatively to the fluctuation of the day, we need to make the most of our personal power.

Let me follow my path today, knowing it's right for me. I will work on letting others walk their own paths, too.

Eternity is called whole, not because it has parts, but because it is lacking in nothing.
> —Thomas Aquinas

We all learn in geometry that the circle is a perfect form, but there's no such thing as a perfect circle. Straight lines aren't perfectly straight; a flat floor can never be perfectly flat. Perfection is an idea that can never be realized.

The idea of eternity is beautiful, like the idea of perfection. It expresses the striving of the human spirit for perfect unity; the fulfillment, the perfect satisfaction, of all desire, perfect wholeness, "lacking in nothing."

Of course, eternity is an impossible standard to attain. Civilizations aren't eternal, nor are laws, nor are works of art. We make ourselves miserable if we try to measure our achievements against such a standard. We invent techniques and gadgets to help us overcome our human weakness and awkwardness. And we cooperate with others, both weaker and stronger than ourselves, to multiply our efforts manyfold. How much kinder it would be to love the idea, as an expression of longing, and to love ourselves because we do the best we can. It's because we lack many things that human beings are so creative and ingenious.

My fullest expression of myself is in my reaching out to others.

December 11

It is not often given in a noisy world to come to the places of great grief and silence.
— Sarah Orne Jewett

Many of us live with energy and gusto, tackling our lives like wrestling partners, busy earning a living, caring for our homes and families, serving our communities. Are we forgetting something?

Often, we forget to nourish our spirits at the deep well of grief and silence. Grief is a nourishing emotion, because in grieving we experience fully the inevitable losses of our lives. Only after grieving can we heal. Only after knowing fully the dimensions of our loss can we summon the vitality to continue our lives.

Parents, friends, children, trusted leaders, die and cannot be replaced. Their loss may have deep meaning for us; we deserve to take the time and care to learn what that meaning may be.

Grief can change people; we may become more detached, quieter, more feeling, more deeply appreciative of life's gifts. One of these gifts is silence—the silence of tranquility. Through plumbing our feelings, we may come to be at peace.

Not all gifts are gaiety, love, and joy. Let me respect the gifts of grief and silence, that I may learn from them.

Pain is inevitable. Suffering is optional.
> —M. Kathleen Casey

Every day is a series of experiences; some we'll greet with relief, laughter, or anger. However, all experiences, even those most dreaded, encompass the very lessons we're ready to undertake. And the people in our lives are here to serve as our mentors.

The pinch of any experience lives on in the mind. We sometimes savor the wound, letting it feed our self-pity or fester our resentment. Likewise, we often hang on to a fond memory, replaying the action over and over again in our minds. Whether it's a good or a bad memory, we neglect the present if our minds are locked in to the past.

Our freedom to let go of an experience, to laugh at ourselves, to accentuate the positive in our lives, exhilarates us. It also heightens our anticipation for every moment a day promises.

I am personally in charge of all my responses to all experiences today. I can feel however I choose every minute of the day.

December 13

Some day science may have the existence of mankind in its power, and the human race [may] commit suicide by blowing up the world.

—Henry Adams

One hundred years ago, Henry Adams foretold a modern predicament, one we all must live with. Science has indeed given us the power to destroy ourselves. How, in such a hazardous world, are we to find serenity?

Peace begins within. Each one of us knows what conflict is, and so each of us possesses the power of reconciliation. The glory of the human spirit lies in our ability to choose, to let go of despair, to turn our energies to creative uses. Peace begins with resolution of our inner wars.

The whole history of our species on the planet has prepared us for the noble choice of peace; it's the fulfillment of our humanity. Each of us must listen to the truth within our hearts; there lies the wisdom we need, and there lies our capacity for love and creativity.

When I listen to the peace within my heart, my spirit is soothed.

The cruelest lies are often told in silence.
— Robert Louis Stevenson

Is it frequent that we fail to come forth to explain, defend, or offer support? Remaining silent is always our option, no matter how grave the situation. Holding back information that would ease another's pain or shed light on a hateful experience is cruel. The effects of cruel acts will find their way back to the actor. The axiom, "As we sow so shall we reap," is true.

Perhaps we need reminding that our performance is unique and essential to those around us. Together we move forward, in concert. When any one of us falters or misses a cue, another of us will likely miss one, too.

We're alive to honor one another's presence, and only when we're fully present, honest, and straightforward are we fulfilling our role.

Today I share center stage. Let me speak my lines fully.

December 15

Eat and carouse with Bacchus, or munch dry bread with Jesus, but don't sit down without one of the gods.
— D. H. Lawrence

In religious communities, as in tribal societies, the ordinary events of life are sanctified. Orthodox Jews and Benedictine monks are alike in this, and so are devout Buddhists, Hindus, or animists. Prayer and ritual observance aren't reserved for special occasions; they accompany sleeping, waking, the daily washing of the body, the simplest meal.

Whatever our beliefs, it's possible for us to express the spiritual dimension of our lives in simple, everyday ways. And each expression strengthens our spirituality and extends it to flood more of our life with light. Whatever names we give to the truths of the spirits, our least act can connect us with them.

The stronger our spiritual connection, the less we'll be held back by our fears and self-doubts. If we can invoke a trusted guide for the ordinary gestures of life, then we'll never lack guidance in perplexity.

I will feed my spirit and it will grow strong.

*Our awesome responsibility to ourselves, to our children,
and to the future is to create ourselves in the image of goodness, because the future depends on the nobility of our
imaginings.*

—Barbara Grizzuti Harrison

The world we live in depends on the responsible contributions each of us makes. And this
world is just as good as are the many talents
we commit ourselves to developing and offering. None of us is without obligation to offer
our best to our family, friends, or strangers, if
our hope is to live in a good world. The world
can only be as good as each of us makes it.

Individually and collectively our power to
mold the outer circumstances of our lives is
profound. Our personal responses to one another and our reactions to events that touch us
combine with the actions of others to create a
changed environment that affects us. No action, no thought goes unnoticed, unfelt, in this
interdependent system of humanity. We share
this universe. We are the force behind all that
the universe offers.

*Whether I acknowledge the depth of my con-
tribution is irrelevant. It is still profound and
making an impact every moment and eternally.*

December 17

Some things you must always be unable to bear.
                                   —William Faulkner

The strong spirit cannot bear lies; the free spirit cannot bear shackles. To tend our spirit with love and rigor means weeding it like a garden, cleaning it of false values and fake pride. We must never bear those things that violate our integrity.

Sometimes, for the sake of peace or a secret doubt that we deserve excellence, we violate ourselves. We give away pieces of our truth and we tell ourselves it doesn't matter. But it does. And we deserve excellence; we deserve the best quality of life. Peace bought at the price of spiritual violation is no true peace; it is a form of oppression.

Meditation can strengthen the spirit against violation. Today and every day, we will practice becoming the person we deserve to be.

When I listen to my own truth I will be guided truly.

. . . I am incapable of conceiving infinity, and yet I do not accept finity. I want this adventure that is the context of my life to go on without end.
—Simone de Beauvoir

The paradox of life is that we cannot conceive of its ending, but we also can't conceive of its not ending. We have the image of the circle to help us out of this dilemma. And if we think of the vast cycles of time and generation, the image of a spiral comes to mind.

The rich web, the adventure of life, goes on without end. It preceded us and will outlast us, and humans will go on struggling and surrendering. A related paradox is that we live in a moment of time that is constantly becoming the past, yet will affect a future that we cannot really predict or control. All we have to work with is our brief arc of life, now.

Yet how precious it is, and how vast, and how it is extended by our ties with others. The web of our relatedness to others brings us into their lives, them into ours. As we share our attention, we enrich our spirits, and we're enriched again by the gifts of others.

A further paradox: every individual is alone, yet none of us is unaccompanied on the curving journey that takes us through this life.

Only by letting go of life do I most profoundly enhance it.

December 19

Gift, like genius, I often think only means an infinite capacity for taking pains.

—Jane Ellice Hopkins

There is no easy way through this life. Few days are void of struggle. Some days are fraught with it. Each day presses us in some manner. Our opportunities for growth, whether on the job or in relationships, are generally accompanied by the pinch of a difficult decision or the push of an unwelcome thought.

Often we need reminding that we're unlikely to attain personal growth without the experience of pain. Pain first beckons and then pushes us forward to new solutions for tired old situations. But these new solutions will always surface if we trust ourselves to move through the pain.

No problem is beyond solving. The process of living, when experienced with care and patience, will reveal the solution that any problem contains.

I will take today slowly and easily. If a struggle develops, I will cherish it. It means growth.

Injustice anywhere is a threat to justice everywhere. We are caught in an inescapable network of mutuality, tied in a single garment of destiny.

—Martin Luther King

Safe in our own homes, or deep into our jobs, it's difficult to remember that we're part of the indivisible life of each, and that everything we do affects that "network of mutuality," just as we're affected by it. Stop and think of the beautiful image of the Arctic tundra, or the atmospheric envelope. These are parts of the world that we may have thought of as inert, nonliving, until we learned how delicate is their sensitivity to everything that touches them.

And everything touches them, as everything touches us. We are as much a part of the rhythm of life as the delicate web of roots that hold the permafrost in place. The same overarching world spirit inhabits us, and we are as necessary as molecules of oxygen.

At last, we have achieved the capacity to communicate with our fellow human beings. Let us hope we can do it as well as sparrows do, or grass does, for we can shape our destiny even as we're shaped by it.

I will try to live today so as to answer for it to all my fellow creatures.

*Now in the middle of my days I glean
this truth that has a flower's freshness:
life is the gold and sweetness of wheat,
hate is brief and love immense.*

—Gabriella Mistral

Eternal truths are always fresh. That's why so many people treasure a daily spiritual guide as an occasion for meditation. Each day we can refresh our spirits with the help of such a guide.

Meditation is a process of simplifying, emptying out, concentrating our minds. We won't achieve much spiritual progress from simply reading these words; they're just the beginning, just the signpost. Growth comes from the work we do, transforming spiritual nourishment into the strength we need.

Some of us are skeptical at first. We don't believe we need to acquire any more disciplines; our spirits are in fine shape, thanks very much. But then we notice a change in our friends or intimates; they've made a discovery. Mysteriously, their lives are straightening out. Maybe we ought to try some of whatever they've got.

It doesn't matter how we come to a program of spiritual growth. The truth was here all the time, waiting for us.

I can't speak the truth too often; it's new every day.

Whensoever a man desires anything inordinately, he is presently disquieted within himself.
—Thomas à Kempis

We are at peace when we cherish the gifts of the present moment. And gratitude for the moment enhances the value of what is to come next. When we take our focus off the present, longing only for another time or place or experience, we'll never reap the rewards that offer themselves to us moment by moment. The longing heart guarantees little peace, infrequent moments of joy, and stunted growth. The soul's nourishment is here, now, with these people who surround us and within these activities inviting our involvement.

So few people understand the benefits of celebrating life as it's received. Finding pleasure in the ordinary occurrences heightens our awareness that indeed, no occurrence is truly ordinary. Every moment is special.

I can answer yes to today and all it offers, and be at peace.

December 23

Women and men in the crowd meet and mingle.
Yet with itself every soul standeth single.
                                        —Alice Carey

Joy for living depends on the level of intimacy with others whom we've grown comfortable with: sharing our grief, our fears, and our glories with others relieves their power over us and fosters a healthier perspective on all the situations in our lives. Yet, even the deepest level of sharing doesn't relieve us of the need to come to full acceptance, solely alone, of the turmoil, the trauma, the tension in our lives.

Interdependently we share this universe, each of us giving to its continuance and receiving sustenance in turn. With little thought, really, we are living our lives bonded in myriad ways, great and small, to one another and to the cycles of the earth housing us all. Just as absolute as is our interdependence, so sure is our need to be at peace. This means to be alone, but not lonely, with our soul's relentless search for understanding, for serenity, for certainty about the direction we are taking. Together and yet alone we are traveling the path of life.

I will find a listener today if I want closeness with someone. And I'll need time alone, away, to understand the life I've been given.

. . . [To] take something from yourself, to give to another, that is humane and gentle and never takes away as much comfort as it brings again.

—Sir Thomas More

We take different kinds of pleasure in giving. Perhaps the purest is the gift to a child so young it doesn't really know who the gift came from; the pure joy that the teddy bear or pull-toy produces is our reward, unmixed by any expectation of return.

When children get older, we want something back from them: gratitude, respect. The gift is less pure. When lovers exchange gifts, their pleasure is often tinged with anxiety: Did I give more than I got? Did I get more than I gave? Or with power: He'll always remember where he got that shirt; she owes me something for the fur jacket.

To friends and relations our gifts reflect many things: our appreciation of their lives, our shared memories, our prosperity. We tend to give in a spirit of *self*-expression.

Perhaps the closest we can come to a pure gift is an anonymous one: a gift of volunteer work, of blood, or a contribution to a charity. Such a gift, which can never be acknowledged or returned by those it comforts, can heal our spirits when they are wearied by too much ego.

The gift of myself can be a gift to myself.

December 25

That life is a fragile shell on the beach I have thought of before. This Christmas I am thinking big basic wonders as if I were just born.

—Naomi Shihab Nye

The big basic wonders about our origin, and that of the stars, must still occur to us all, even though we're grown up and knowledgeable about astronomy and human reproduction. The germination of a seed is still much more wonderful, in a strict sense, than the mere electronic marvel of a calculator that makes twelve thousand computations in a second.

Do we ever let ourselves simply wonder? Do we still open ourselves to the awe that filled us once, when we first realized the vast intricacies of the solar system or of human physiology?

Every great ritual surrounds a story that is wonderful: the presence of a god; the deliverance of a people; the transformation of life or death. It's appropriate that we should respond to them with a thrill of wonder. Wonder is a gift; it contains the germs of reverence and of knowledge.

Life is frail and intricate, and it contains everything I need for fulfillment.

A holiday is a permitted—or rather a prescribed—excess, a solemn violation of a prohibition.
> —Sigmund Freud

Breaking our own small rules is a luxury that we sometimes forget to indulge. How pleasant it can be to stay in bed late on a Sunday, not get dressed or shaved, to let clutter accumulate. On our days off, we can get a thrill from such "solemn violations" as going to a film in the afternoon, eating an unscheduled treat, jogging twice around the track.

It's probably important to give ourselves these little extravagances, especially if our usual lives involve a highly organized routine. Just breaking up the day differently—reversing daytime and nighttime activities, for example—can give a special flavor to a day off.

Routine is consoling for many of us. We feel good about ourselves as long as we keep to the schedule, obey the rules. But we need to break some rules to get a different kind of good feeling about ourselves; above all, to know that we can choose to return to our former law-abiding selves. Sometimes we fear that if we step out of line once, we'll never get our lives together again. We need to know that we can renew ourselves on a holiday.

Giving myself a holiday by breaking my routine can make it stronger—because I choose to resume it.

December 27

Anger repressed can poison a relationship as surely as the cruelest words.

—Joyce Brothers

Anger toward a mate, a co-worker, a friend, or neighbor, builds a strong wall, separating us from everyone if we don't acknowledge the cause of the anger. Like any secret, denied anger festers and infects relations with friends, acquaintances, even strangers. It dominates our attention and pollutes every emotion. But more importantly, if not checked it controls us, and this all-consuming power then decides our destiny.

Anger doesn't need to be a major force in our lives. Like any emotion, we can learn from it, but we must let it go if we are to grow. It helps to remember the sweet aftertaste when an angry encounter is resolved.

Anger acknowledged and resolved tightens understanding between people, and encourages intimacy. Anger is bittersweet when squarely faced.

My anger need not own me today.

How magnificently you tossed away this God who plagues and helps man so much! But you did not and could not toss out of your heart that part of you from which the God notion had come.

—Richard Wright

Each of us accommodates "the God notion" in our own way, but we all have it. Although we may not all worship a great Mother or Father figure, our spiritual dimension makes us all kin.

To deny our spiritual selves will bring us unrest; our life's journey is always toward serenity, and serenity means finding peace within, answering those searching questions of the spirit. Some of us will seek answers in many forms, in different languages, but our quest is as real and as simple if we stay at home and explore within ourselves.

When we're honest with ourselves, we find this radiant truth: an authentic search for spiritual wholeness can be successful.

Let me honor "the God notion" and never use it against myself or any fellow being.

December 29

The way in which we think of ourselves has everything to do with how our world sees us and how we can see ourselves successfully acknowledged by that world.
> —Arlene Raven

Our self-perception determines how we present ourselves. The posture we've assumed invites others' praise, interest, or criticism. What others think of us accurately reflects our personal self-assessment, a message we've conveyed directly or subtly.

It behooves us to acknowledge the power we each master over others' judgments and opinions of our worth. It's with absolute certainty that those opinions are molded by our own. When our personal opinions are negative, it's likely to be because we've lost touch with the rhythm of this life we're sharing with others. Perhaps we've forgotten what is essential to the completion of the whole. Perhaps a gentle reminder is needed, day by day.

How I grade myself today will he imitated by the men and women who share my experiences. I can earn high marks if I want to.

. . . Is not all the world beyond these four little walls pitiless enough, but that thou must need enter here—thou, O Death?

—W. E. B. Du Bois

The concept of a refuge strengthens us. For some of us, it's a dark basement and headphones, or a workbench; for others, a garden or a bedroom.

Some of us take refuge outside ourselves, in our spiritual faith. There we find a death-defying certainty and a reminder that our being is a gift. Some of us find this refuge in service to others; we feel the benign power of creation stream through us, and we're strengthened.

Death is part of life, and it belongs on the same plane as life's other events: birth, nurturing, and sickness. But spiritual refuge lifts us to another plane, where the powers of life and death join to form the whole of existence. This higher truth, like all real refuge, lies within us. We can summon it as the need arises.

The more I turn outward to others, the stronger I become within.

December 31

Despite my geographical love of mankind, I would be attacked by local fears.

—Grace Paley

We may have the highest principles, be generous, trusting, and public-spirited, and still find ourselves assailed at times by doubts and fears. The "local fears" don't mean that we've betrayed our "geographical" principles; only that, this time, we're afraid.

The wonderful thing about being human is that we can choose how we act at any given moment. If we find ourselves behaving in a way we don't like, we can choose to change; either to change our behavior or—if that doesn't seem possible—to change the way we look at it. It's wisely said: "You can do something for twelve hours that you could never think of doing your whole life long."

It's a waste of time and effort to disapprove of ourselves. If we won't change our behavior, let's change our standards. Many of us have impossibly high expectations for ourselves, and when we don't measure up, we feel guilty.

Guilt is unproductive. When we keep everything in the moment—the "geographical" as well as the "local"—we can accept ourselves as we are. We are as good, right now, as we can be.

Scaling down my expectations closer to what I'm capable of will aid my spiritual growth.

SUBJECT INDEX

AUTHOR INDEX